Cultural Chemistry

CULTURAL
CHEMISTRY

Simple Strategies for
Bridging Cultural Gaps

Patti McCarthy

First published 2016
Cultural Chemistry

Diagrams by Ian Scott
Typeset by BookPOD
Cover image © iStockphoto

Disclaimer
The material in this book is general comment only and neither purports nor intends to be specific advice related to any particular reader. It does not represent professional advice and should not be relied on as the basis for any decision or action on any matter that it covers. To the maximum extent permitted by law, the author and publisher disclaim all responsibility and liability to any person or entity, whether a purchaser or not, in respect to anything and of the consequences of anything done by any such person in reliance, whether in whole or in part, upon the whole or any part of the contents of this publication.

A Cataloguing-in-Publication entry is available from the National Library of Australia

ISBN: 978-0-9946441-0-7 (paperback)

eISBN: 978-0-9946441-1-4

To my parents, for giving me itchy feet and to my husband David, for helping me to scratch them.

Join the Conversation!

If you have a favourite cultural moment to share, or a story in this book jogs a memory, please share it! Perhaps you would like to post a photo of yourself, reading this book in some exotic location?

You can join in the conversation on Facebook at
https://www.facebook.com/CulturalChemistrytheBook/

You lost me at 'Hello'

You lost me at 'hello'. From the get-go our relationship was doomed to failure, as you knew nothing about my culture, could not speak a single word of my language and were only interested in a short-term, money making exercise.

You lost me because you tried to shake my hand when my religion doesn't permit me to do so. You lost me when you just took my business card and put it into your back pocket, without reading it. You lost me at our first meeting, when you proceeded to call me by my Christian name, as though we were old friends.

You lost me when you failed to join my team at lunch, when you didn't repay the hospitality I showed to you when you visited my country and when you opened my gift in front of other people. You lost me when you referred to my wife as the hostess and again when you sat with the soles of your feet facing me.

I had such high hopes of expanding my business to another country, but you lost me by failing to understand how much these small things matter. Just because it doesn't matter to *you*, doesn't mean it doesn't matter.

Patti McCarthy, LinkedIn post, April 2015

Contents

Chapter 3
First Impressions

Chapter 4
'But I thought you Said...'

Chapter 5
Ant or Colony?

Chapter 6
Wrong Direction
Management & Motivation Differences........................... 109

Chapter 7
All in Good Time
Time & Planning Issues 131

Chapter 8
Lucky for Some
Superstitions & Magic 153

Chapter 9
Etiquette Matters
Appearances & Hierarchy...................................... 169

Introduction

Why Should You Read This Book?

It can be extremely stressful being out of your comfort zone. As a business traveler or as an expatriate, you quickly become aware of cultural differences and you suddenly realise that getting the contract signed and even keeping your job may depend on getting things right.

If you have ever been a client, colleague, employee or host from another culture, you may have experienced cultural 'gaps' such as;

- starting your sales presentation with a joke which nobody laughed at.

- leaning in for a kiss on the cheek when somebody offered you their hand.

- being offered a gift and not having one to give in return.

- being convinced your deal is in the bag, but walking out empty handed.

- not getting what you ordered in a restaurant.

- clearly causing offence, but without understanding why.

- being unable to motivate someone from a different country.

You already know, therefore, why you need to read this book, because it was highly embarrassing or confusing then and you don't want to have to go through that again. Because nobody had told you then that these things were important and now perhaps you are worried about what else you don't know...

Why Did I Write This Book?

Quite simply because over the years, *so* many people have said to me 'You really ought to write a book about all these things' – so here it is.

However, this isn't just a book about cultural differences. Of course, this *is* a book full of examples and stories about cultural differences, but it's also a coaching based approach to how you personally can manage them, because that seems to be the missing piece for so many of the expatriates I have worked with. Moving overseas or starting to work with clients or colleagues from 'somewhere else' should not be approached with a 'business as usual' mindset, as all parties would benefit from;

- Learning more about the cultural differences.

- Anticipating and accepting that where there are differences, there will be issues.

- Understanding how to *manage* the differences more effectively, how to create and be comfortable with a 'new normal', how to succeed in spite of or even because of the differences and how to ride out the frustrations and focus on the rewards.

There are already a number of great books about cross-cultural differences and I have referred to many of them in this book, but there aren't many which actually help the individual to respond more positively and more openly to those differences, to work with them instead of fighting against them. What this book aims to provide therefore, is useful information about cross-cultural differences, but combined with some suggestions about the way those differences might make you feel and some strategies for having a more positive approach.

What Equips Me to Advise You?

I'm what's known as a '3CK' – a third culture kid – and cultural differences have always been a large part of my life. My parents were both English, but I was brought up in England, Belgium and the USA and I have spent time living in Botswana, Singapore and Australia, as well as travelling widely. My sister married an Italian, my brother married a German and I married someone of Irish descent; my mother used to refer to us (*very* tongue-in-cheek) as "the Wops, the Krauts and the Micks." My husband and I have three children, all born on different continents. It was somewhat inevitable that cultural differences would become a passion of mine.

Sadly, after working for ten years as a cross-cultural coach and trainer, I know that for many people cultural differences may be fascinating, but they can also be enormously frustrating. *Cultural Chemistry* is therefore, first and foremost, a very practical guide to making sense of these differences and understanding both why it goes wrong sometimes and what can be done to get it right. It is by no means a totally

> I know that for many people cultural differences may be fascinating, but they can also be enormously frustrating...

comprehensive journey through all the cultures in the world, or the many differences that there are between them, but it is a start.

> The first thing you'll learn about is the **Four R's,** a simple but logical model I have created for anticipating and becoming more comfortable with potentially sticky situations.

The first thing you'll learn about is the **Four R's,** a simple but logical model I have created for anticipating and becoming more comfortable with potentially sticky situations. It will help you to not just successfully manage cultural differences, but actually learn to enjoy them and ultimately, to thrive in whatever new cultural situation you may encounter. I will then detail a number of strategies for you to employ, as part of the **Four R's** approach and in the rest of the book, we'll look at some of the most frequent causes of 'cultural gaps'. These include differences in verbal and non-verbal communications, in leadership and motivation styles, in office etiquette, in client servicing and much more. At the end of each chapter, you have the opportunity to consider how the **Four R's** could be applied to the situations described and to reflect on your own, similar experiences.

Gurnek Bains writes in *Cultural DNA* that 'Global CEO's need to become cultural experts, psychologists and historians if they are to make the right long-term calls for their companies' and it isn't just CEO's who need to do this. Anyone wishing to have a rewarding and enjoyable exchange with people from another culture, cannot just ignore cultural differences. You can't pretend that they don't matter, or hope they will go away if ignored for long enough. You will reap far greater rewards by gaining an understanding of how things are done there, as opposed to insisting on doing things your way. Getting things right may take a little more preparation, but as any good builder knows, it is better to spend time building good foundations than repairing cracks.

Barriers to Success

We are all foreigners to somebody, bringing with us our values and our expectations and we are *all* potentially quite difficult to deal with at times. Context has a lot to do with how we handle challenge too; the gaps are always wider when people are stressed and anxious. When we are on holiday and our train is running to what the Indonesians call 'jam karet' (rubber time) it's annoying, but not usually serious. When we are trying to get to Jakarta for a meeting and the guard can't tell us *what* time the train will arrive, our tempers can start fraying much more quickly.

> Context has a lot to do with how we handle challenge too; the gaps are always wider when people are stressed and anxious.

Some of our stress response is also due to what Buddhists call 'attachment to ego' or in other words, worrying that we will look stupid. As stress levels rise, thinking reverts to a mixture of arrogance and ignorance; this is when we become adamant that our way is the best way and that anyone else's way is incorrect. It's easy, in this state, to take the cultural hiccups personally and begin to feel that people are deliberately blocking us or making our lives difficult.

Another contributing factor is ethnocentrism, believing that our cultural values and mores are inherently correct and that other ways of doing things are not only weird, but plain wrong. When we look at people from different cultural backgrounds, we tend to look through the lens of our own culture and what we 'see' is often distorted by our own values. We see certain things, we interpret them according to our values and we jump to conclusions – often in error. Viewing the behaviour of others from our own cultural perspective can distort reality, the way that fairground mirrors can give us giant heads or extra-long legs. We see things that 'don't look right' to us because they are different from the way we would do it, such as somebody saying yes but meaning no, accepting criticism for something their colleague did or wanting to rewrite the terms of a contract after signature.

For many Westerners, for example, the wearing of a burka indicates oppression rather than an expression of modesty. Saying yes but meaning no can be seen in the West as duplicitous, rather than as a means of maintaining harmony. Silence in response to a question is assumed to mean a lack of understanding, rather than the possibility that someone is taking time to consider their response. Instead of exploring the why behind the what, we make an assumption based on the way *we* would do things. A deliberately gentle handshake from a Thai man might suggest to Westerners a lack of confidence. Comprehension and language problems might be construed as a lack of intelligence and a young Vietnamese woman giggling behind her hand might be viewed as foolish, rather than shy.

Similarly, for many Asians, an American boss asking his or her junior for their opinion may suggest to them that the boss is not as smart as they should be. South Americans who happily combine business and social relationships could find it odd that their British colleagues don't invite them to dinner and an Indian manager may be frustrated that his Australian team won't answer his non-urgent emails over the weekend.

Self-awareness

Recognising our tendency to see things through the perspective of our own cultural lens is critical for anyone hoping to successfully navigate cultural gaps and is an important element of the **Four R's**, which we will discuss in the next chapter. When we understand how and why we got it wrong last time, we will understand how to get it right next time – or at least how to try. Cultural gaps will not be bridged overnight, but if we are willing to have a few missteps along the way, it will be well worth the journey.

Recognising our tendency to see things through the perspective of our own cultural lens is critical for anyone hoping to successfully navigate cultural gaps...

As Dutch cross-culturalist Fons Trompenaars so aptly describes it in his book *Riding the Waves of Culture*,

> We need a certain amount of humility and a sense of humour to discover cultures other than our own; a readiness to enter a room in the dark and stumble over unfamiliar furniture until the pain in our shins reminds us of where things are.

Different doesn't need to be difficult. The **Four R's** approach cannot solve every issue and it cannot replicate real life experience, but my aim is to give you the confidence and the strategies you need, for at least trying to bridge the cultural gaps which you find yourself teetering on the edge of. And this book is not, of course, a totally comprehensive journey through all the cultures in the world, but it is a good place to start. It is hopefully not as daunting as the reading list of one hundred books I was given at school, with the title 'A Reading List for those Who Would Like to Start to Become Well-read'.

> Culture is like a river, it is always changing and always evolving, so we have to keep exploring it.

Culture is like a river, it is always changing and always evolving, so we have to keep exploring it. We will almost certainly never have all the answers, but I hope this book gives you the interest and the motivation to keep looking for them.

Apologies...

Navigating cultural differences is not without risk, so I apologize unreservedly if I have caused offence to anybody, or resorted to stereotypical or generalized descriptions which somebody might find offensive. Also I am myself a Westerner, being English by birth, so my Western perspective may sometimes creep in, but I have tried very hard not to commit either of these offences.

All the stories and anecdotes told in this book are either my own experiences, those of my clients or those of people I have met over the many years of working in this area. I have also heard and read many examples of people falling into cross-cultural gaps, through the books I have read on the subject and the discussions I have enjoyed with global colleagues on LinkedIn and other sites. All names and places of people featured in the anecdotes have been changed. I have used the terms 'Anglos' to specify those people from English speaking Western cultures and 'Westerners' as a more general term.

While *Cultural Chemistry* is written primarily for a business audience, it will I hope be enjoyable for anyone with an interest in cultural differences. Although most of the anecdotes are from business situations, I have indulged my passion for cultural differences and occasionally included anecdotes which might not be strictly relevant in a Fortune 500 boardroom, but which I thought were worthy of telling because they were so interesting.

Enjoy!

References:

- Gurnek Bains, *Cultural DNA*, Wiley, New Jersey, 2015 pp. XI
- Fons Trompenaars, *Riding the Waves of Culture,* Brealey, London 2011

Introducing the Four R's

Becoming more aware of and more comfortable with cultural differences is not an 'opt in' any more. For any individual or any business who hopes to work seamlessly with clients from many different countries, it is an essential requirement. So, where to start?

Consider while you are reading how easily so many of the difficult situations described could have been avoided with a little forward planning, tolerance and patience. All of these qualities and more are needed if we are to truly embrace and enjoy cultural differences and I have bound them together in a simple, but effective four-step approach which I call the **Four R's.**

The four steps consist of Rewards, Research, Reflect and Reach Out.

Note that none of the **Four R's** refers to either 'Respect' or 'Rocket-science'. Many people would argue that respect is the cornerstone of any successful cross-cultural interaction, but I believe that if you haven't done your research and therefore lack knowledge, you don't understand *why* someone does something. Without this back story, it is much more likely that you will find that behaviour 'difficult' and you will therefore be less likely to be *able* to respect it.

Take, for example, the habit of saying yes but meaning no, which many Westerners find one of the most baffling traits they encounter when working with people from Asian countries and which is discussed further in Chapter 4. If we understand that for people from Asian countries, maintaining harmony is one of the most important cultural drivers, we can start to appreciate why this happens. If we add to that knowledge the fact that most Asian societies are very high context and that meaning is conveyed in far more than just words, we start to understand that we need to 'listen' for far more than words. If our Japanese host or business colleague smiles gently at us, looks away, asks us to remember another occasion on which we met and says regretfully that what we are asking for "might take some time", it must be understood that is the equivalent of an Englishman's emphatic "over my dead body!" – but stated with the delicacy that the Japanese prefer.

Let's go through the **Four R's** step by step.

Step 1: Rewards

What's in it for you?

We are all motivated by rewards, whether tangible or intangible. Why do *you* want to learn about cultural differences? What benefit will you get? What's in it for you?

- Maybe you feel that your product could be hugely successful in an overseas market, but you need a local partner to work with you.

- Perhaps there is a colleague or member of your team whom you feel has great potential, but whom you sense is not fully engaged.

- Perhaps there is a client or a supplier whom you find very abrasive and annoying and you'd like to improve that relationship.

- Maybe there is the chance of an expatriate assignment in the future and you would like to demonstrate your suitability for the role.

- Or maybe you are simply going on holiday somewhere new and you want to learn a bit about their customs and language.

> **Research shows that people who have clear goals, that have been written down, are more likely to achieve them.**

There are multiple reasons for wanting to become more culturally informed and determining what your motivation is will help to drive your learning. Research shows that people who have clear goals, that have been written down, are more likely to achieve them. It may be quite easy to 'fall off the wagon' and decide it is all a bit hard and you can't really be bothered, but if you write down your goals in terms of *how specifically* becoming more culturally aware will be an advantage to you, it should be an incentive to keep going.

More than anything, you have to *want* to improve your skill set in this area. Like dieting, or any behavioural change that requires an effort on your part, you have to drive this change and be motivated by the outcome. If you are not interested, don't see the point and can't really be bothered, then perhaps you should give this book to a friend instead – but do be aware that the rest of the world will be moving on without you.

Step 2: Research

What do you need to know and why?

One of the biggest causes of stress is feeling out of control; when we work across cultures and things don't proceed as we expect them to, we can feel vulnerable and exposed. Get the control *back* by becoming informed, so that you won't be taken by surprise. Whether you are going to another country on business or pleasure, or the person you are about to meet there is going to be your manager or your client, do a bit of homework first. There are thousands, if not millions of words of advice available on the internet, probably almost every question you have can be answered – but will you think to ask them? The single most common problem I encounter in my work, is not that people are deliberately ill mannered or ignorant, but that **they simply don't know what they don't know.** It doesn't occur to them that things might be done differently 'somewhere else', they keep doing what they've always done – sometimes with disastrous results.

> We only have one chance to make a first impression and if we don't get it right, we can waste a lot of time trying to fix it.

We only have one chance to make a first impression and if we don't get it right, we can waste a lot of time trying to fix it. Consider these kinds of dilemmas that can rapidly turn hot prospects into dead ends;

- When you meet your Nigerian client for the first time, will you know how to address her?

- When your French client invites you to lunch, will you know when is the right time to start talking business?

- Will you treat your Japanese client's business card with enough respect or will you be politely shown the door – or even blacklisted for 50 years, as one French company supposedly was.

- When meeting with your Singaporean client, will you know whether to address your technical questions to the MD or the Technical Director?

- When your Omani client invites you to his home, will you try to greet his wife and daughters with a handshake?

- When your Filipino supplier asks to see a photo of your partner, will you think that's inappropriate?

So often we approach cross cultural situations in a state of 'cultural cruise control'; assuming that our way is the only way and that everyone else will act like that too. But if other things in the culture are different – the food, the clothing, the climate, the language and the lifestyle to name just a few very obvious things – it is highly unlikely that the cultural values which drive behaviours would be the same too. Taking even just ten or fifteen minutes to do a little research will make you aware of the most important 'Do's and Don'ts' and could save you hours in the long run.

A list of recommended further reading and of useful websites can be found at the back of this book. You can also simply type 'business culture in (name of country)' into your search engine and plenty of links will come up, some inevitably more valuable than others. Most importantly, use your network; find a colleague or friend who has perhaps lived in that country, or worked with people from that country and ask them for some insights and advice.

Step 3: Reflect

How do you feel about what you've learnt?

Reflection or self-awareness is a critical step, as without it your research can only take you so far. Culturally intelligent people can interact effectively with people from many different cultural backgrounds and recognize that it is not a one-way street, but a continuous loop, requiring each party to respond to the other.

Having done some research into the other person's culture, you may feel that there are significant differences between your culture and theirs. You may indeed start to worry about how you will cope with the differences, but you also need to think about how the other person will cope with *you* and your odd ways. Don't forget, *they* think *you* are the different one! What we say isn't always what is heard, and our usually successful efforts at getting to know people – making some small talk or breaking the ice with a joke, for example – might fall on very deaf ears, if people don't understand you or don't think your behavior is appropriate.

If an American, for example, learns that the Japanese business people she is meeting with are most likely to be hierarchical, collective and quite reserved, she needs to carefully consider her approach. Suggesting to them that using first names in the office is going to be easier, insisting that everyone's opinions are important and emphasising that she wants them all to be honest and say what they really feel, is likely to get a very different response from her new Japanese colleagues than it would from her American ones.

Reflecting can also be thought of as being 'mindful' and it can be a lot harder than it seems. Much like the fish who doesn't realise how comfortable it is in the water until it's flapping on the bank, we are all so accustomed to doing things our way that we do them without thinking. If you think how hard it is to brush your teeth with your non-dominant hand, you start to get an inkling of how hard it can be to switch off our default behaviour, but it is a crucial step towards having a rewarding cross cultural relationship.

So, how *will* you connect?

Step 4: Reach Out

How can you make a meaningful connection?

If you really didn't have time to do any research and have not yet learnt the art of self-reflection, you can and must at least practice this step. Reaching Out is about recognising that you and your colleague may be standing on opposite sides of the street – or possibly of a multi-lane highway – and that you need to find a new way to connect. What bridges can you build? What strategies can you employ to help cross the gap and ideally, meet in the middle? Reaching Out is about being prepared to compromise, to be flexible and to be willing to bend towards the middle to offer a helping hand; it is NOT about selling out your own culture or trying to be someone that you are not.

Note that while I favour compromise wherever possible, I absolutely don't believe that you should lose yourself in the process of becoming more like the other. The reality is, though, that in an expatriate or visitor situation, there will inevitably be one or few of you who is uncomfortable and many more of them who are perfectly happy. Expecting the majority to change would be naïve, so the onus falls very clearly on the newcomer to understand the laws of the land and adapt accordingly.

> The French have a great expression which I refer to often; "In every relationship there is one who kisses, and one who offers their cheek."

The French have a great expression which I refer to often; "In every relationship there is one who kisses, and one who offers their cheek." It describes perfectly the unequal relationship between the giver and the receiver, or the buyer and the seller and nowhere is it more appropriate than in cross cultural dealings. Imagine that two people try to sell you the same item, for the same price and in all other ways exactly the same – which one will you buy from? The one who is completely different from you or the one you feel a little more comfortable with, because they seem a little more like you?

It isn't racist to opt for the latter, it is human nature to feel a bit more comfortable and confident with someone who seems a bit more like 'us'. So, if we are dealing with people who are perhaps not like us at all, we have to try very hard to *create* commonalities where perhaps naturally there were none. People make their minds up very quickly about whether they feel comfortable with someone or not; we only have one chance to make a first impression and we can spoil it pretty quickly by something as simple as not having a reciprocal gift, addressing someone incorrectly, asking them to sit in the wrong seat or refusing a local delicacy. This is why Research pays off.

Recommended strategies for Reaching Out and bridging those cultural gaps are detailed in the next chapter.

Applying the Four R's

In Chapter 1 the **Four R's** approach to cultural differences was introduced and we discussed what the four steps entailed. At the end of every chapter, you will be asked to consider how using the **Four R's** might have been beneficial to some of the individuals you will have read about, or perhaps to you personally if you have experienced a similar situation. But for now it is only about you, so please take a few moments to answer the following questions before continuing. You might also like to revisit these questions when you have finished reading the book and see if your answers have changed at all.

Rewards

Questions: What are some potential rewards for you? A new client you want to grow, an overseas trip, a promotion? A challenging relationship you hope to resolve by reading this book? What goals do you have in mind, that becoming more aware of cultural gaps and how to bridge them will help you to reach?

Considerations: _____

_____

_____

_____

_____

_____

Research

Questions: What kind of research would be helpful for you to undertake? What do you need to know and what do you need it for? Are you wanting to entertain your new German clients, understand the buying habits of young Chinese mothers or know how to behave with your new Thai in-laws?

Considerations: _____

_____

_____

_____

_____

_____

Reflect

Questions: What things about your own behaviour might
you need to consider changing? Ask your
friends and colleagues for their honest input
and also make a point of comparing yourself to
others. Are you a talker? Do you talk quickly and
interrupt people frequently? Do you take up a
lot of space in the room? Jump to conclusions?
Add two and two and get five? Aim to always
close the sale? How well will these behaviours
go down with the people you hope to connect
with?

Considerations: _____

_____

_____

_____

_____

Reach Out

Questions: What kind of strategies do you use at the moment to try and connect with people from a different cultural background? Currently, do you do anything differently when you meet people from a different culture? Having answered the Research and Reflect sections, you may well be thinking that some of your communication strategies could do with an overhaul. What changes might you need to make?

Considerations: _____

_____

_____

_____

_____

Are there any other things to consider in light of what you've learnt from this chapter?

_____

_____

_____

_____

_____

2

Strategies for Reaching Out

We are all foreigners to someone and every country is complicated to the people unfamiliar with it. Of course, some people will just crash through the cultural barriers, but when we attempt to connect with someone from a different culture, most of us will feel a bit unsure of ourselves, as though we are walking on thin ice and wondering if it will give way at any moment.

Part of what's happening is that we are moving from a state of unconscious competence to a state of conscious incompetence.

Almost any learning follows this pattern and in the area of cultural differences it works like this;

- **Stage One, Unconscious Incompetence.** In which we don't even *think* about it. We don't know what we don't know and we don't really notice or mind if we get it wrong. Unfortunately, some people may stay in this state forever, but others will recognise their shortcomings and seek to transition out of this stage.

- **Stage Two, Conscious Incompetence.** At this stage, we are aware that we are doing things incorrectly and we don't like it, but we don't know how to get it right! This motivates us to learn about the differences, so that we can feel more comfortable and we transition again.

- **Stage Three, Conscious Competence.** By now we have done some research and have a good idea about how to behave, but we have to keep thinking about it and we are constantly reminding ourselves that what comes naturally might not be appropriate and that what feels awkward might be perfect.

- **Stage Four, Unconscious Competence.** Finally, the last step; when it all comes naturally and we wonder why we ever found it so difficult. When we are both familiar and relaxed with cultural differences and most of the time we can actually get it right, without having to constantly think about it.

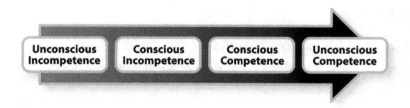

The way we experience this in 'real terms' is that previously, we never really thought about the way we did things, we just did them. We didn't have to think about it, as we somehow just knew what was the right thing to do. If we were from a Western country, we rarely took our shoes off at the door, we knew what to wear to a Black Tie event and we knew not to burp at the table after a meal. At work, we knew what management tools worked for us and what didn't and we knew how to establish friendly relationships with our colleagues. Hopefully, we never stopped being willing to learn, but we usually knew how to communicate with and motivate our team and we understood how much guidance to offer, without fear of being viewed as interfering or micro managing.

If we were from Asia, on the other hand, it is very likely that we would know that the way to succeed at work was to never disagree publicly with our boss and to carry out instructions in a diligent and careful manner. On the whole, we would be most comfortable wearing the same sort of clothes to work as everybody else and generally fitting in with the crowd; if we were singled out by our American boss as *Employee of the Month,* we would probably be highly embarrassed. We would never eat our lunch in front of our computers.

Suddenly we find ourselves living in a different culture, where people *do* take their shoes off at the door and we are embarrassed by having holes in our socks. Where we're actually not sure *what* the dress code is for dinner at our boss' house and where he may indeed surprise us by burping his appreciation after the meal, but be offended by our referring to his wife as the hostess. Imagine it from the point of view of a young Japanese employee, who has a new Australian boss in Perth. His manager wants him to demonstrate initiative and work independently, so she doesn't give him much guidance, even though he'd really like some. And although she leaves quite early in the evening, she never seems to stop during the day, so he's not sure if he's allowed to go out for lunch. She's also asked him to call her by her first name, but that feels really awkward for him – he wasn't even allowed to share an elevator with his boss in Japan. It is all *very* confusing for him.

We all want to be able to build friendly, comfortable and successful cross-cultural relationships, but it can be surprisingly difficult to do. Although wanting to do the right thing is hugely important, being willing isn't enough on its own, we need to combine that drive with bridging strategies that are known to be effective.

The Reach Out strategies listed below are a great place to start;

Turn off Your 'Cultural Cruise Control'

Your 'cultural cruise control' is much like the cruise control feature in your car; it allows you to stop thinking consciously about the ways in which you interact with people and to proceed with little interruption to your 'business as usual' approach – often at high speed. This has got to be your number one strategy, as cross-cultural dealings are *not* business as usual. You will need to be very aware of 'other drivers' and will need to slow down to read all the warning signs.

Build Rapport

Being culturally intelligent is about being aware of the differences and to some extent celebrating them, but at the same time being able to focus on what we still have in common – despite the differences. Rapport can be used to *create* commonality, by subtle matching of body position, eye contact, speed and volume of speech – even breathing rate. Without being obvious, observe the other person; how are they sitting, how loud is their voice, how regular is their eye contact, how often do they smile at us? What can we change about how we are sitting and talking, to make ourselves

> Being culturally intelligent is about being aware of the differences and to some extent celebrating them...

more like them? Making repeated eye contact with someone who looks away every time we catch their eye is not a happy experience for either of us, so be prepared to also change your thinking about what might seem to you to be your open and friendly demeanor.

Nearly all of us are more comfortable being with people who are *like* us, (which explains a lot about the predominance of unconscious bias) and rapport allows us to create the illusion that we are actually quite similar, even if we are not. If we are both leaning forward with one hand supporting our chin, both speaking at the same speed and the same volume, both making regular eye contact and both drinking coffee, our brains see us as 'the same'. The brain doesn't differentiate between reality and perception, so if it *looks* like we are getting on, the chances are that we *are* getting on – and we can all start to relax a bit. Part of the trick, of course, is that if we are so busy focusing on what we have in common, we are too busy to think about what is different. If this all sounds like too much hippie-talk, just try it – you'll be amazed.

What you will also notice, once you start thinking about it, is how naturally you get in rapport with someone whom you already know and like. I often find that when telling people more about my work, and particularly when we start talking about the importance of building rapport, I can point out to them that *we are actually already in rapport*. Just the fact that our heads are aligned, often leads our bodies to align too.

Support ESL Speakers

We tend to talk predominantly about ESL (*English* as a Second Language) issues, although of course on many occasions people need to learn other languages too. As native English speakers, It will certainly help with acculturation if we can learn to speak at least some of the local language, but it is not very likely that anyone would be expected to work in it, as English has without doubt become the language of business. It is *the* second language to learn and it is *the* language that everyone uses when they need to have one language in common in an international group.

This has not only created problems for non-English speakers, it has also led native English speakers to be complacent, thoughtless and often downright selfish. Because English is the dominant language, there is little motivation to learn another one – other than to meet school requirements or for pleasure. This means that many English speakers have absolutely no concept of how challenging it is to conduct business in a second language. The effort of having to keep up with colleagues using jargon, abbreviations, metaphors and idioms – let alone talking quickly and frequently interrupting each other – is enormous. If we think of the mental challenge we face when having to drive on the other side of the road, we can get some feel for the issue. If we also changed the traffic light colours to purple, blue and white, had circular STOP signs and the brake and accelerator pedals switched over, we are definitely getting closer.

> **Those of us with English as our first language often have no idea how lucky we are, while people with English as a second language (ESL) are reminded of it every day.**

Those of us with English as our first language often have no idea how lucky we are, while people with English as a second language (ESL) are reminded of it every day. Being the dominant language for both business and tourism, we make the assumption that wherever we go, someone will speak English and while that certainly isn't always the case, it very often is. The burden of bridging the communication gap falls fairly and squarely (actually, not fairly at all) on the shoulders of the non-native English speaker, who must work far harder than us simply to keep up, let alone get ahead. Can you conceive of how fluently you must be able to speak that second language if you are expected to be able to communicate sophisticated ideas in it?

Claudia was very excited about moving from Milan to London. She had always got good grades in school and was comfortable taking part in meetings run in English, when any of the English managers came to visit. In London though, it was a different matter. She realised that group meetings in Italy had been easy because like her, everyone was speaking a second language, but in London she was often the only one. She found it very hard to keep up and quite unable to contribute, although in Italy she had always been very vocal and was known for coming up with creative solutions. After only two weeks, she felt far less self-confident and not sure at all that she was really ready for this move.

As well as being difficult, it is also extremely tiring working in another language all day. Many people, whether they are waiters or doctors, au pairs or engineers, arrive in the English speaking country as Claudia did – believing that they speak English quite well, because they have performed well under exam conditions. Once they get into real-life situations, however, it becomes a whole new challenge that is both stressful and exhausting. Most newcomers will also be keen not to appear difficult, or to draw attention to themselves, by asking people to repeat or rephrase themselves. Misunderstandings arise, perhaps mistakes happen and the newcomers' confidence is rapidly eroded, leaving them even more anxious.

So, how can you help? Think how good it would be for everyone, if communication were more straightforward. Record and listen to yourself on the phone one day, preferably when talking to someone with ESL; how often do you use metaphors or abbreviations? Do you

> Record and listen to yourself on the phone one day, preferably when talking to someone with ESL; how often do you use metaphors or abbreviations?

speak slowly and clearly? Does your voice get louder as you strive to make your meaning clear? It really doesn't help to SHOUT! Do you use jargon and slang? In what ways do you check that everything has been understood and what feedback loops do you have in place to ensure that it really has? Do you emphasise that it's fine to come back to you, if anything isn't clear?

Doing more to support ESL speakers is a real win-win situation that will pay huge dividends for any investment made. See Chapter 3 for further thoughts on ESL issues.

Learn to Listen

For many Westerners, a conversation is like a tennis match; a question or statement comes over the net and has to be responded to straight away, to show that we are on the ball. Many Westerners also listen in 'waiting to talk' mode; we listen – perhaps a little impatiently – to what the other person has to say, so that they will then be obliged to listen to us – which we think of course is no hardship, as what we have to say is *far* more interesting!

For many people from the Middle East, Africa, North and South East Asia, this mode of listening is both confusing and rude, as their speech pattern is much more like gently rolling a lawn bowls ball and waiting to see what course it takes. This is not to say that Asian people have no purpose in their speech, far from it, more that conversations have a more elastic quality that happily accommodates greater thinking time, without in any way suggesting that somebody is lost for words.

This type of conversation pattern is referred to as 'Active Listening' and the Chinese character used to write it, shown below, incorporates the ears, eyes, heart and attention. Active listening involves listening both patiently and attentively and in responding, using the speakers' words back at them by weaving them into our own speech. If answering a question, we deliberately and obviously take time to think about our answer before giving it.

EARS

EYES

UNDIVIDED ATTENTION

HEART

For those more used to active listening, when someone responds with too much alacrity it suggests that they haven't thought much about the question. Failing to use their words back at them implies that the person hasn't understood them properly or wasn't really paying attention. A true exchange of active listening is like a beautiful braid, which picks up different strands of conversation and weaves them into a neat whole. It is a mannerism which benefits everyone, for we all love to feel that we are interesting and that we have something to contribute.

Ask, Don't Assume

I once saw a sign in an office which read "To Assume is to make an ASS of U and ME". This is rarely deliberate, but unfortunately it is often the unintended outcome, as Paul found;

Paul was the American Managing Director of a public relations company in China. His firm had landed the account of a large ice cream company and Paul thought it would be a great PR stunt to take free ice cream to all the patients in the local children's hospital. He canvassed the idea with his team and was met with rather weak smiles and – to Paul – a surprising reluctance from anyone to volunteer as the organiser of the event. Enthusiasm didn't really improve over the next few days and it was only when the Chinese client looked unhappy that Paul questioned his idea and learnt that in Chinese culture, it was seen as unhealthy to give cold food to sick people.

> It's impossible to know everything about a culture; even if it is our *own* culture we can't know it all, as culture is continually altering and developing.

It's impossible to know everything about a culture; even if it is our *own* culture we can't know it all, as culture is continually altering and developing. A river is always made of water, but depending on tides, weather and multiple other factors, the content of the river and the quality of the water will change constantly – and so it is with culture. What we have to get better at doing, therefore, is reflecting on our tendency to make assumptions and recognise that our knowledge is almost certainly limited. We will make the most progress when we are prepared to be humble, to ask lots of questions and to be genuinely willing to learn.

Cross-cultural books are full of excruciating mistakes that other people made, whether with their dress, their behavior or their efforts to sell their products. Incorrect translations have caused many a red face too, as in Japan, where somebody agreed to signage declaring 'Welcome to the f*&#ing sale!' all over the shop frontage. In Spanish, 'no va' means 'it doesn't go' but Chevrolet and Vauxhall didn't think to check this before marketing their

'Nova' car in South America. And in the former Yugoslavia, a somewhat confusing sign was spotted in a hotel lobby, which read "The flattening of underwear with pleasure is the job of the chambermaid."

As an expatriate family, we have had many experiences like this. The Belgian removalist assisting my parents advised my mother that it was "customary to give gratification to all Belgian removal men", while my sister confounded the lovely woman at the local dairy shop in Milan by asking for yoghurt without 'preservativi' (condoms) instead of 'conservanti' (preservatives). My Father told a waitress that he had left the poubelle (rubbish bin) on the table, instead of the pourboire (tip) and I told a German doctor that I had been bitten by a flying horse, rather than a simple old horsefly.

On a more serious note, there are a number of international mergers and acquisitions which have failed spectacularly and the lack of cultural considerations is seen as a key factor in many of these failures. In 1998, Daimler-Benz acquired Chrysler for US$38 billion and sold it to Cerberus Capital nine years later, for almost US$30 billion *less*. As reported on the Commisceo Global website;

> It was this failed partnership that first rang the alarm bells that cultural factors just cannot be ignored on a global level, especially not within mergers and acquisitions...Analysts agree that the cultural gap in corporate cultures was one of the main reasons for the Daimler-Chrysler failure. Daimler was a German company which could be described as "conservative, efficient and safe", while Chrysler was known as "daring, diverse and creating. American and German managers had different values which drove and directed their work. Different departments were heading in opposing directions.

No amount of cross-cultural training or research can fully vaccinate us against these cultural blunders, but asking rather than assuming will significantly improve the odds in our favour.

Engage Your Inner Sherlock

Learning about cross-cultural differences doesn't require you to put on a Deerstalker and smoke a pipe, but it does make discovering considerably easier if you seek out your 'Inner Sherlock' and engage willingly in playing the detective.

Having considered the Rewards of getting it right the first time, be prepared to spend time doing the Research and have a good idea of what to expect. If you know that you are visiting Iran, for example, you will learn that as a man, you are forbidden to touch any woman who is not related or married to you. You need to then Reflect on your default behaviour; is it to shake hands, kiss someone on the cheek, put your hand on the small of someone's back as you usher them through the door? These are all absolutely forbidden, so you will not only have to avoid doing them, but also have to think about what you can do instead, to still feel that you are behaving politely.

Enjoy the learning opportunity, see what you can discover about the culture that you didn't know before. If you have time, read a novel by a local writer or read through some blogs written by other people living there. Go and see a film from that country or find out about tourist destinations and places of national pride. Ask colleagues if they have experience of working there or if they know someone who does. In many ways, becoming more culturally intelligent just starts with *expecting* difference, long before you start to learn about what those differences are.

Mark is an architect, who says part of his 'detective work' when he travels overseas is to challenge himself to notice what is different:

"I'm fascinated by cultural differences," he told me. "It's a bit of a game to me to see what differences I can spot. As soon as I hop into a taxi, I look around to identify some things that are done differently to my normal," he says.

"Is there a statue of a Hindu deity on the dashboard for example? What language does the driver speak? Are most people well or poorly dressed? Is their clothing bright or dull? Are there any shrines? Are the shops open at this time and what are they selling? What are the displays like compared to home? It's amazing the things we start seeing when we start looking!"

Mark says he can play this game for hours and he finds it really helpful to draw his conscious attention to all these differences, as once he is aware of them, it instinctively makes far less sense to expect 'business as usual.'

As well as being smart, it's also both polite and friendly to take a little time to learn about someone else's culture – and hopefully they will do the same for you. In our home in Melbourne, we are Airbnb hosts and have enjoyed the company of visitors from many different countries. We have found that taking the time to learn even a little about their culture before they arrive makes people feel both welcome and special.

It is really important that in the process of observing all that is different, you *notice,* but you *don't judge.* It is almost automatic to fall into thinking right and wrong, good and bad and so on, so be aware of this tendency at

> It is really important that in the process of observing all that is different, you *notice,* but you *don't judge.*

all times. Behaviours typically evolve because it works for those people in that situation; being 'wrong' for you does not make it wrong.

Be Honest

In my training courses I often show a picture of a set of teeth with a little bit of spinach wedged between them. I ask how many people would like to be *told* if they have spinach in their teeth and usually most of the participants put their hands up. I then ask how many of them are comfortable *telling someone else* that they have spinach in their teeth and usually less than 20% respond.

This is one of the biggest challenges with working across cultures; most of us want to get the chemistry right, but we feel uncomfortable both telling others that they got it wrong and asking for help ourselves. Clearly this is a no-win situation! If someone's behaviour makes us uncomfortable, it is far better to very politely come clean and explore the issue, rather than ignore it and hope it will go away. Remember that most people (perhaps ourselves included) have not done their Research. They don't know that they are upsetting us and we may not even understand *why* their behaviour upsets us so much. *We both don't know that we don't know and this is potentially a very dangerous situation for everyone!*

If I do something wrong today and my colleague offends me tomorrow and we both hold back on helping each other, then neither of us will learn anything. So, if we want to learn, we have to get more comfortable with saying 'I'm sorry, I don't quite understand what happened here, can you please explain?' Don't forget to also preface the request with a comment to the effect that honesty now will be much appreciated and for you, will be far less painful than making the same mistake again. And if someone is humble enough to apologise to you for getting something wrong, be sure to accept the apology with good grace and no grudges held.

Bend or Snap

Young trees have the ability to bend in the wind, so that they are not snapped in half by strong winds. Skyscrapers too have some movement built into them for the same reason and when working across cultures, it is essential that we adopt some flexibility too.

The definition of 'flexible' in the Cambridge Dictionary is 'able to change or be changed easily according to the situation.' We do this in order to reach a compromise, defined in turn as 'an agreement in an argument in which the people involved reduce their demands or change their opinion in order to agree.'

If only it were as easy to do as it is to say... But compromising is not about giving up or giving in, but finding a different path to perhaps a slightly different solution. If we insist that once signed, contracts cannot be modified, we may find working with Chinese clients to be extremely frustrating. The Western view of a contract as being the final step in the process is not shared by the Chinese, who believe that if, for example, the price of shipping goes up after the negotiation, it is only fair to increase the price to the buyer. We may not be able to change their point of view, but at least if we are aware of it, we can build flexibility into our pricing and we will be justified in demanding a few modifications of our own.

> Compromising is not about giving up or giving in, but finding a different path to perhaps a slightly different solution.

Amanda experienced some challenges in the Middle East, which required her to compromise on her usual style;

> *Amanda worked in the travel industry in the UK and had recently begun dealings with a Saudi Arabian client. Having travelled to places like Dubai on holiday, she felt that she was quite familiar with the culture, but in meetings she was frustrated by her clients' obvious refusal to accept her as the senior member of the team. Despite being impeccably courteous to her, their questions were always addressed to her junior male colleagues and her contributions to the discussion were largely glossed over.*

Should Amanda's company have just accepted it and sent in a man? It should not be necessary, as if we know that something like this is likely to happen, we can plan a strategy with our colleagues that helps us to achieve our objectives. In Amanda's case, it was important to position her as the senior lead, so her team was asked to call her 'Mrs. Smith' in front of the client, instead of 'Amanda'. All questions asked of anyone except Amanda had to be referred to her, either to answer herself or to give permission for them to answer. Clearly these behaviours would not have gone down at all well in the UK, but were an effective compromise strategy that could be adopted temporarily.

Note that this type of situation does not always arise; many Western women have no issue at all when working in the Middle East, although in many cultures there is often some other hierarchy at play whether age, gender, qualifications or connections. A colleague told me of a female Sri Lankan sales rep who worked for a pharmaceutical company; in Sri Lanka she was frequently ignored in favour of the Australian male field manager, until customers were told that she had a PhD, at which point they promptly turned their backs on *him*.

Avoid Stereotyping

Many people are dismissive of both stereotypes and generalisations, but they are not the same thing. Personally, I feel that generalisations can be a very good entry point into learning about a new culture, in much the same way that a roadside sign warning of 'curves ahead' advises us of potential danger. The sign itself won't get us round the bend, only safe driving will do that, but it will make us slow down and *anticipate* the corner.

Generalisations work in the same way. They are based on what is generally known to be true about a nationality – that the Italians are quite passionate, the Japanese are extremely polite and the Indians very spiritual, for example – and help us to sort people into some kind of grouping. The problem with generalisations is not that they are necessarily wrong, but that they are incomplete; they are jigsaw puzzles with pieces missing from them and it's up to us to remember this. Generalisations are simply a starting point. At the very least, they do prepare us for things to be *different* and hopefully suggest to us that we turn off our cultural cruise control. We clearly shouldn't expect all people from that culture to behave in a particular way, as Brendan, an American, learnt when he relocated to Italy;

Brendan had spent some time learning about Italians before his relocation to head office in Rome and he was feeling quite nervous. He had read that Italians scored highly in both Uncertainty Avoidance (dislike of ambiguity) and Masculinity (highly success orientated) on Hofstede's Cultural Values Index and he was wondering how this would play out for him. His own style was just to 'have a go' and this had worked well for him in the USA and on visits to Australia, but he was worried that his Italian colleagues might feel that his approach was risky. It turned out that he need not have worried; while many of the administrative staff seemed to love planning and detailing, his senior colleagues were much more open to taking a calculated risk. The Italian generalisation that Brendon had uncovered certainly applied to some Italians, but by no means to all.

Stereotypes, on the other hand, tend to be far more pejorative and limiting and are based on things assumed to be true, rather than proved to be. They limit people from fulfilling their potential and can be very damaging to society in general, but also to our own relationships with individuals. Stereotypes usually spring from an absence of personal experience and knowledge and are often based on someone's else's message, such as a political party or media outlet who may have more self-serving motives. Those who promote these messages can be particularly adept at creating and promoting stereotypes, such as that all people seeking asylum are 'queue jumpers' or that all women wearing short skirts are 'asking for it'.

Don't Take it Personally

This last strategy will almost certainly be challenging for most people. When we are used to being successful, to people liking us or admiring the way that we do things, it can be extremely galling to suddenly find that we have somehow lost our touch. Remember the fear of looking stupid that was discussed in the previous chapter? This is exactly what happens when we are caught unawares and the usual response is to blame the other person, rather than to blame ourselves. To assume that 'they' are being difficult, that they are stupid, rude, backward – whatever adjective springs to mind – and that we are without fault.

Barbara moved from Madrid to Melbourne, to join a large bank. We spoke on the phone several times and after three weeks, met up face to face. Barbara seemed very miserable; she told me that her Australian colleagues were not friendly, that her move to Australia had been a big mistake and that she should never have come.

"Australians don't like me!" she declared hotly. "And I don't like them! Coming here has been a disaster!"

What upset Barbara was that nobody had invited her out to coffee or lunch, in order to get to know her a bit better. In Spain, this is what happens, this was Barbara's 'normal'. There is a high degree of overlap between people's work lives and private lives in Spain and she had expected that colleagues would at the very least have invited her out for lunch and very possibly have invited her to their homes too.

However, instead of either asking me or her colleagues (in an indirect way) whether this was the norm in Australia, she *assumed* that the lack of invitations meant quite clearly that they didn't like her. In other words, she took it very personally when it wasn't meant that way at all and she made relationships strained and awkward when they didn't need to be.

This type of resentment will obviously not help to build positive and rewarding relationships, so try very hard to view the situation objectively. If this happened to someone else, would you still think it was a big deal? Do you really think that the other person intended to slight you, or could it be that they don't understand your way of doing things either? Taking things personally is unfortunately very natural, but it is hardly ever warranted and is a massive waste of energy and emotions. Don't go there!

Applying the Four R's

In this chapter we have discussed the way in which we progress from ignorance to knowledge and from incompetence to competence. We have also explored multiple ways in which you can Reach Out to people from other cultures, including being more supportive of ESL speakers, building rapport, switching off your cultural cruise control and engaging your Inner Sherlock. By all means, add your own methods and strategies to this list.

While this chapter has mostly been about strategies for **Reaching Out**, the other three R's have also had a part to play. Think about:

Rewards

Questions: In what ways do the Reaching Out strategies also reward you?

Considerations: In a nutshell, they make your life easier – a huge Reward. They make communication more straightforward, make you feel more confident, make you appear more considerate and equip you to connect with all kinds of people. Can you think of some specific situations in which you could – very soon – use some of these strategies to solve a problem or to progress a difficult situation?

Research

Questions: What Research could Amanda have undertaken in preparation for her trip to the Middle East? What kind of enquiry will be most helpful to you, in doing your Research?

Considerations: Amanda could have explored various internet sites, hired a cross cultural coach to brief her, sought input from colleagues within her organisation or even from her LinkedIn community. There is always someone, somewhere, who has the answer to our question and the bigger challenge is recognising that we need to ask it. Remember, business in another country is rarely what you expect it to be.

Reflect

Questions: Consciously Reaching Out to others inevitably heightens your own self-awareness too. What do you think others might say about you? Next time you find yourself speaking to someone who has English as a second language, what adjustments might you consider making to your own speech?

Considerations: Do you really have a good level of self-awareness or do you just think you do? Think about whether you can feel the same enjoyment when working with someone from another culture and if not, try to uncover why this is. Ask how other people view your connectivity skills and don't resent them for telling you if you have spinach in your teeth.

Are there any other things to consider in light of what you've learnt from this chapter?

_____

_____

_____

_____

_____

References

- http://www.commisceo-global.com/component/easyblog/cultural-differences-in-international-merger-and-acquisitions, quoting research by Appelbaum, Roberts and Shapiro, 2009:44)

- https://geert-hofstede.com/national-culture.html

- Geert Hofstede, *Culture's Consequences*, SAGE Publications, California,1984

3

First Impressions
The First Five Minutes

There are so many small ways to get it wrong. You can have all the information at your fingertips, offer the keenest price and the best service, but if you get it wrong in the first few minutes, it can sometimes be very difficult to climb back up from that. Handshakes, the exchanging of gifts, the handling of business cards, where you sit and what you do with your hands may not be an issue for people interested in a merely transactional exchange, but for those wanting to build a longer-lasting relationship, these are all key indicators of your suitability as partner material. Many of the Reach Out strategies will have a big impact in the first five minutes too, especially getting in rapport, practicing active listening and engaging Sherlock. Falling at this first hurdle may mean that you will miss out on the race altogether.

It's in Your Hands...

Handshakes can very quickly send the wrong message. In Australia, a strong handshake is seen as a sign of strong character.

Men in particular are expected to greet other men with a firm handshake and on many occasions my own hand has been inadvertently crushed in a large paw. In Thailand, Indonesia and Sri Lanka, to name just a few countries, strong handshakes are seen as aggressive, so men's handshakes are expected to be much more gentle – often just a placing of their hand in the palm of the other person's.

In many traditional Australian Aboriginal societies, the handshake may last for several minutes and consists of a light but firm pressure, during which a person's energy is sensed and energy is exchanged. Many white Australians are uncomfortable with this handshake, especially as it is not respectful in some Aboriginal cultures to also be making strong eye contact with an Aboriginal person. Everything you may have learnt in your Western culture about how to greet people – firm handshake, warm smile, lots of eye contact – is suddenly all wrong.

In other cultures, women do not shake hands at all. In South East Asian countries, many women will press their palms together and incline their heads in a small bow called a *wai*, a *sampeah* or a *sembah*, depending on the country. While this is considered to be an expression of femininity, men will also do this gesture occasionally (not usually to Western business people) as it originates from a gesture of friendship, used to show that nobody is holding a weapon.

In the Qur'an it states that *all* Muslim women are prohibited from making bodily contact with a man who is not either their husband or their relative, but obviously not all women will follow this instruction to the letter. In fact, both Muslim women and men prefer to avoid physical contact with people who are not close relatives. In early 2016 a secondary school in Switzerland initially gave permission for some male Muslim students to *not* have to shake hands with the female staff, as was the local custom. This led to much debate in the European media, including the BBC, about whether these boys should be expected to fit in with local customs, or whether it was simply a sign of the acceptance of religious differences to allow these cultural preferences to be respected. In media reports on the situation, one Islamic spokesperson confirmed that this action *is* prohibited, although another said that it was not. In the end, in response to local outcry, the school did rescind the permission and the boys are now expected to shake hands as all other students do. The story is a good illustration of how a simple gesture that Westerners may take for granted, such as offering someone a hand out of the car or patting them on the shoulder, may be not just completely unwelcome but could be cause for affront.

In a similar vein, a Western skincare company had an interesting experience when it opened some stores in Japan. As part of both making the customer welcome and allowing the customer to experience the product, the sales consultant will offer to wash and massage the clients' hands. While this ritual is very popular in many other countries, in Japan it is less so, as it is felt to be too intimate an exchange to take place between strangers.

Seeing Eye to Eye

How much eye contact to make is often a concern in cross-cultural situations. Eye contact is one of the first actions that

> Eye contact is one of the first actions that people notice and judge each other by in a first encounter.

people notice and judge each other by in a first encounter. However, 'the norm' varies hugely across cultures and just like some other non-verbal communication, it has the potential to be truly inappropriate and downright offensive.

In researching this chapter I came across an American website called *Art of Manliness*. Authors Brett & Kate McKay recount how research reveals that people who make a lot of eye contact are perceived by others as 'more dominant and powerful, more warm and personable, more attractive and likeable, more qualified, skilled, competent, and valuable, more trustworthy, honest, and sincere and more confident and emotionally stable'. Wow!! And if that weren't enough, by *not* making eye contact you are perceived as 'hiding deceit, masking emotions and insecurity'.

It's tempting to rush up to someone and immediately start making eye contact, but as the author acknowledges, 'the importance of eye contact ... can vary from culture to culture'. Indeed it does, to the extent that the same action can have two different interpretations, depending on where they take place. So while in North America, Europe and Australia, making eye contact implies that you are warm, personable, confident and so on, in many Asian, African and Latin American countries, making eye contact suggests that you are aggressive, challenging and rude. In these cultures, far from 'hiding deceit, masking emotions and insecurity', avoiding eye contact is considered highly appropriate behaviour between people of different hierarchical levels and suggests that you are – you guessed it – warm, personable and confident!

Jaime and Frank had enjoyed an 'on-line' work relationship for the last six months. Frank, from Ohio, was sales director for the USA and Canada and Jaime, a Brazilian, had joined the team six months ago as sales manager for Central and South America. The pair regularly exchanged emails and had developed an easy relationship; fortnightly phone calls often lasted longer than they needed to and Frank found he was sharing quite a bit of personal information with the younger man about some issues he was having with his teenage son and his wife's recent breast cancer surgery. The annual sales conference was coming up and Frank was really looking forward to actually meeting Jaime in person, as he felt they had a real connection.

When they finally met up face to face, Jaime was indeed still warm, but Frank found him somehow more evasive than he had expected. He felt embarrassed by how friendly he had been to Jaime, but couldn't put his finger on what had changed until his colleague Rob commented 'Jaime seems like a decent guy, but I never feel quite comfortable with people who don't make eye contact, do you?' That was it! Because Jaime wouldn't maintain eye contact with him, Frank found it hard to trust him. His old man had brought him up to believe that an honest, confident man will always look you straight in the eye and that value was hard-wired in him.

The problem was, Jaime's dad had brought him up to show respect for older and more senior people by not making strong eye contact. Jaime was very grateful for the extra help and indeed the friendship that Frank had shown towards him, but he was concerned now that he might have been a bit too friendly. He thought he had better pull back a bit and demonstrate the appropriate level of respect for him.

Indeed, the very qualities that some Americans find admirable (assertiveness, power, strength) are actually seen as undesirable in a number of other places, including Japan, Sweden, Rwanda and Costa Rica. In many cultures, being too powerful implies an unwillingness to seek the input of others and to compromise and generally it is not appreciated. The African 'Big Man' concept discussed in Chapter 6 is a notable exception to this.

While people from many English-speaking and European cultures are generally comfortable with sustained eye contact, even they can find it a bit intimidating if someone tries to hold their glance too long. Supposedly, holding eye contact for more than six seconds in any culture means that you either want to have sex with or murder that person! In nearly all cultures, prolonged eye contact can be suggestive of sexual desire – initiating it meaning 'I'm interested', and returning it meaning 'I am too'. In the Middle East, men will make eye contact with other men to demonstrate their trustworthiness, but eye contact between men and women is limited to a very brief flicker in order to avoid this type of situation.

Exchanging Gifts

To the Japanese, presenting a gift at the beginning of your relationship clearly demonstrates your intentions and indicates the value which you place on the relationship. The gift will be thoughtfully chosen and beautifully presented; the giver will hand it to you with two hands and a slight bow and it should be accepted in the same manner. The other person should then offer their gift, similarly beautifully presented, but neither party will open the gift in front of the other, to avoid possibly shaming the other by having bought a more expensive gift.

At least, that's how it's supposed to work … More often, a gift may be offered but the wrapping looks tawdry next to the beautiful Japanese gift. Sometimes the gift is just accepted and put to one side without much care or obvious gratitude. Worst of all, sometimes there is no gift at all, sending a message to the Japanese host that as far as you are concerned, it's all about the deal and very little about the personal relationship.

Research would quickly tell the potential business traveler that the exchanging of gifts is an extremely important courtesy to the Japanese. When staying at Airbnb's in Japan, we were often given gifts by our hosts of small boxes, packets of paper and so on. It is not unusual for people to come up to you in the street and give you small pieces of Origami they have made and the group of middle-aged women on our hiking trip in New Zealand last year seemed to have an endless supply of tiny embroidered ornaments to give to everyone they met.

> It is not unusual for people to come up to you in the street and give you small pieces of Origami they have made...

Often, however, people know what to do – but that doesn't mean they really buy into it.

> *Belgian executive Jean-Luc had worked as a CEO in Japan and confessed that he found the whole bringing of gifts and 'face time' to be a real nuisance. His failure to appreciate the value of face time for his Japanese clients and the reward that it gave them, is a perfect example of a frequent business traveler with extensive global experience, who nevertheless lacks cultural intelligence in the true sense of the word.*

Business Card Etiquette

The mistakes that occur over the exchange of gifts also occurs with the handling of business cards, which in most South East Asian countries are to be treated with the utmost respect. As with the gift, the card should be offered and received with two hands; in the case of the card, with two thumbs resting lightly on the corners. The writing on the card should be facing the recipient – preferably in his or her language, with your language on the reverse. The card must then be carefully considered and either placed on the table in front of you, or carefully tucked into the shirt pocket, 'closest to your heart', as the Chinese like to say. It should *never* be just casually tucked into a shirt or trouser pocket without a second glance and never *ever* put into a back hip pocket and sat on! I always suggest to clients that they respond as though they have been given something really beautiful, which they want to spend time looking at, but 'Josh' didn't quite grasp this;

> Barry was visiting a company in Japan with his American colleague Josh. As a long-term resident of China, Barry was very familiar with the etiquette around business cards in Asia and had tried to ensure that Josh appreciated how serious it was, but he was a bit worried. Sure enough, about 45 minutes into the meeting, Josh was starting to look impatient at the – by his standards – pedestrian pace of the meeting. He started playing with the Japanese man's card, firstly tapping it on the table, then doodling on it and finally absent mindedly picking his teeth with it.
>
> Needless to say, they didn't win the business.

Business cards are about far more than just giving people your contact information. In China, for example, where one's *guanxi* is critical, the card is extremely useful. (*Guanxi* is loosely equivalent to 'network' or 'connections' and is discussed further in Chapters 5 and 9). The card provides a person's job title (something many Western companies are moving away from), qualifications attained and sometimes their place of study. This not only allows the recipient to pigeonhole the owner of the card and rank

Business cards are about far more than just giving people your contact information

them according to status, it also provides a talking point and an opportunity to comment to the person, by saying for example 'I see that you attended Nanjing University, I hear that has an excellent engineering department'. Such is the importance of business cards in China that they are exchanged regularly in social settings too.

This type of behaviour might be seen as obsequious in many Western countries, but not so in Asia. Indeed, the failure to treat the card with respect and again, as with the gift, failure to observe the local courtesies, can make a very bad first impression on someone who is quite confident that *their* way of doing things is how all well-mannered people behave.

Personal Space

If you search 'personal space' on Google Images, a photo comes up of a man wearing what looks like a bicycle wheel around his waist. It keeps other people on the street at a prescribed distance away and the wheel seems to be rigid, so nobody can get too close. People from many Asian countries have an invisible 'bicycle wheel' around them, but they take theirs on and off, depending on the circumstances.

At a business function in London, Mary found herself chatting to three businessmen from Korea, Malaysia and Japan. They stood in a diamond pattern, but slightly too far from each other for Mary's comfort, so she stepped towards the Korean man, thinking that the others would also step in closer. Instead, as she stepped forward, the Korean stepped back and the other two also moved, so as to maintain the same distance from each other. Mary tried a couple more times, but she was outnumbered and simply found herself in an elaborate four-person waltz!

In most Western cultures we tend to be quite comfortable standing about half a metre apart, but in most Asian countries and amongst Indigenous Australians, a metre is a much more comfortable distance and if you try to step closer, they will step back. I have sometimes even seen people pushed up against a wall by an enthusiastic networker with little sense of personal space. On the street, however, as anyone who has visited Hong Kong or Beijing will know, it is fairly common for people to bump into you and just keep going without apologising – presumably because the streets are so crowded, you would not have time to apologise to everyone.

Not stepping into someone's personal space is primarily a demonstration of respect in many cultures. Especially in a business context, it is not appropriate to get too close to people you hardly know or who are more senior than you. When people from Anglo, Mediterranean and Latino cultures pull their chairs up right next to people from these countries, pat them on the arm or put their arms around another's shoulders, many less demonstrative people feel that their space has been somewhat invaded. On the other hand, in non-business settings, getting physically close to someone is a sign of friendship and being open. In many African countries, for example, people will sit right next to you on a bench or in a cinema, despite there being plenty of empty seats around to choose from. Meaghan also observed this while living in China;

> Not stepping into someone's personal space is primarily a demonstration of respect in many cultures.

When we complained to our Chinese friends about often feeling 'crowded out' in restaurants, they told us that Chinese people often feel more comfortable when they aren't far away from others. This explained why, when we'd choose a quiet table in a corner of an empty restaurant, inevitably the first tables to be taken by the next few patrons to come in would be those right next to ours. We couldn't figure it out, as in Australia, you'd usually go for a quiet, private table rather than choose to sit right next to the only other people in a restaurant. Quite a few friends told us that Chinese society is so crowded and noisy that they felt unsettled if they found themselves in quiet, empty settings. I found that explanation made a lot of sense!

Body Talk

Public displays of affection (PDA's) are generally frowned upon in countries such as Japan, Vietnam and most of the Middle East. PDA's between the *same* sex are, however, a different matter and in countries such as Vietnam and Cambodia, many Western men feel slightly uncomfortable at the sight of heterosexual men demonstrating their friendship by holding hands.

Miles was on a bus in rural Thailand many years ago when he felt a hand creeping up his legs which, unlike those of Thai men, were covered in dark curly hairs. A hot-blooded young man at the time, he wasn't overly worried until he saw that the hand belonged to a very elderly man, who had clearly never seen such hairy legs before!

Touching out of curiosity is considered to be fair game in less developed countries, although clearly this is unlikely to be a problem you will encounter in a business meeting. Whilst travelling in Southern Africa in the 1980s, however, not only did my mop of blonde hair earn me the name 'Lion Woman', but people often felt entitled to stroke it and even to pull strands of it out.

Muslim women wear a hijab or other head covering so that seeing their hair is a privilege reserved for their husband and traditionally, Sikhs do not ever cut their hair, but wear it wrapped up in a turban. As Western ways prevail this is becoming less common, but for those who do observe this tradition, it is very meaningful for them and of course, very personal. Not everyone is as culturally intelligent as they could be, however…

A French friend, Stephanie, told me of a very clumsy exchange between her Sikh colleague and her German colleague, which took place in the company's New Delhi office. The German man, on the first meeting with the Sikh man, not only asked how long his hair really was, but if he could see it sometime. He then went on to ask if the Sikh fellow also observed the rest of the five articles of Sikh faith, known as the '5 K's' and if he wore a specific style of cotton underwear called Kachera under his robe!

It's great to be interested in other people's cultures, but there is a time and place for everything.

Hindus and Buddhists believe that a person's spirit or soul resides in the head, therefore it is a sacred area that nobody is allowed to touch. While you are unlikely to stroke the hair of your Hindu colleague in a meeting, you may be invited to their home and a simple act such as ruffling the hair of their small child could upset people. Head movements are responsible for many misunderstandings too, especially when an assumption is made that 'yes' and 'no' are expressed the same way. For hundreds of years in Western cultures, the inclination of the head was interpreted as a sign of submission or agreement, so a nod came to mean 'yes'. A Westerner shaking his head from side to side, however, doesn't always mean 'no'; sometimes – if he is smiling too – it means 'I can't believe it!' An American

> **Hindus and Buddhists believe that a person's spirit or soul resides in the head, therefore it is a sacred area that nobody is allowed to touch.**

nodding her head up and down usually means 'yes', but in Greece, Macedonia and the Balkans, an up-down movement with an emphasis on the *up* is a definite 'no', while a side-to-side movement means 'yes'. Indians are known the world over for their famous 'head bobble', a combination of up and down and side-to-side movements, which can mean 'yes', 'no' and everything in between and which only Indians are fully able to both deliver and interpret with confidence.

At the other end of the body, the sole of the foot is considered one of the dirtiest parts of the body and as such, in many African and Middle Eastern countries, it is considered very rude to show or point the soles of your feet towards someone. In many Asian countries, touching anyone with your feet is also offensive, so keep feet tucked under your own chair and don't stretch long Western legs out under the table. If you do inadvertently play footsie with or kick another person under the table, place your hand on their arm if possible and apologise profusely. Be aware that even when crossing one leg over the other, the sole of your foot may be facing your neighbour, which would be insulting.

It's hard to believe, but when I was discussing these issues on a radio program once, an Australian man rang in to tell us his experience with this. A regular visitor to Thailand himself, he was aware of the etiquette around feet, but he had taken his Thai client to meet a colleague in another office, who clearly was not. The colleague had apparently leant back in his chair and put his feet up on the desk, with the soles facing the Thai client. As the caller said, it took a very long lunch to iron that one out.

Talk to the Hand

Another issue to be conscious of is hand gestures. As with eye contact, the *same* gesture can mean different things in different cultures and you may not get the outcome you intend. The right action will support what you are saying, but the wrong one can create real confusion. And, of course, if we lack words and instead try to communicate without them, making the right gesture is even more important. Imagine your confusion if someone were smiling broadly at you, but at the same time signaling that you should get lost?

> Imagine your confusion if someone were smiling broadly at you, but at the same time signaling that you should get lost?

The common 'thumbs up' gesture is often a source of confusion, as it means 'OK' or 'good' in many Western countries, but in Turkey, Iran and Buenos Aires it has distinct sexual connotations. Similarly, the 'A-OK' sign (thumb and forefinger in a circle, remaining three fingers pointing upwards) which is widely used in North America, is regarded in South America as an invitation to have sex and in Turkey as meaning that you are worth a big fat zero.

In Australian Indigenous cultures, beckoning someone with your forefinger is considered equivalent to waving your penis at them, and you will struggle to hail a taxi in Singapore unless you point to the car with a flat hand, palm facing downwards and curl you fingers into your palm to beckon them. In many African cultures, pointing with your finger is considered aggressive; instead, people point with the chin and also roll or widen their eyes in the relevant direction.

Philip's experience in Vietnam is definitely one to take note of;

Philip was happy with the way the meeting had progressed in Hanoi. He had asked a couple of colleagues who had worked in Vietnam before for some etiquette tips and he was pretty sure he hadn't made any huge blunders. His client smiled at him as he reached for the contract and said he felt confident that the deal would go well. "Fingers crossed!" said Philip, showing his two crossed fingers to Danh, whose smile froze on his face.

In Vietnam, crossed fingers represent a woman's genitals and as such were clearly an inappropriate sign to make on the signing of a contract.

In France, simply snapping the fingers of both hands at the same time can be cause for offence, while in Russia, while shaking hands is common, it must never be done in a doorway. The 'talk to the hand' gesture, so common amongst Western teenagers, originates from a Byzantine gesture known as the *moutza*, Still widely used in Mexico, the Middle East and parts of Africa it basically conveys a dislike of what the other person is saying and a wish for them to stop talking. Allowing the hand to do the talking is far less confrontational than using words.

In Western cultures, a discreet look at your watch is accepted code for 'I have to be somewhere …' and most people will not take offence at it. While of course sometimes you do have a deadline, in the Middle East and South America especially, it is considered rude to look at your watch while speaking to someone. The belief is that the conversation should take as long as is needed, for everything of importance to be said.

Applying the Four R's

It's rather worrying how quickly people make their mind up about you, isn't it? And that what you *say* accounts for far less than what you look like and the way you behave. In seeking to engage across cultures, getting these behaviours right is even more critical, as people usually have very firm ideas about what is appropriate and what isn't. There is a body of scientific research supporting the validity of 'trusting your gut instinct' and Malcolm Gladwell's book *Blink* explores this in detail. As you will have seen from the stories in this chapter, however, the idea that you can always trust your gut should really come with a caveat: **This may not apply in cross-cultural situations**.

How would you apply the **Four R's** to these issues?

Rewards

Questions: Are meetings with new clients from different cultures sometimes harder than you expected them to be? Are your cross-cultural encounters often not as rewarding as you would like them to be? Do they sometimes leave you feeling that you haven't quite connected?

Considerations: Remember how much our behavior accounts for, especially when combined with ESL issues. Are you fully prepared? Be sure that your expectations are in line with the degree of challenge that you face in doing business across cultures. This isn't 'business as usual', it's often difficult, frustrating and tough on your confidence. Cut yourself a bit of slack, but also recognise that there are significant gaps in your knowledge and set about filling them. The more you increase your competency, the more enjoyable these encounters will be.

Research

Questions: If you know that you will shortly be meeting with a potential client from Malaysia for example, what do you need to Research in order that the first five minutes go as smoothly as possible? What kind of things will help you to manage any differences that arise?

Considerations: Think specifically about a situation that you suspect will arise, given what your research tells you. Are you comfortable with how to respond? Do you know whether to look your client in the eye or not? Does it make any difference if the client is an older woman? Many of the issues in this chapter could have a bearing on your meeting.

Reflect

Questions: Thinking about your answers to the Research question, what might you need to change about your own behavior? How well can you build rapport? How comfortable do you think you make people feel? Why do you think some people don't mind bumping into you on the street but insist on standing an arm's length away from you in the hallway?

Considerations: Think about the reaction you get when you put your arm along the back of someone's chair, or pat them on the shoulder to imply 'well done'. Notice whether you are always chasing eye contact, or if it happens naturally. Think about how you feel when you want to earnestly impress a point on someone, but they keep stepping away from you.

Reach Out

Questions: Rapport is critical in the first meeting and many of the issues discussed in this chapter – including eye contact, personal space and business card etiquette – will be addressed by paying attention to it. When you are talking to people, do you like to touch people on the arm, maybe put your arm around their shoulders, shrug emphatically, raise your arms in disbelief? Or maybe you are keen on hand gestures – thumbs ups and tapping the side of your nose and so on – but do you always know what your hands are saying?

Considerations: For many people, expansive hand gestures can convey passion and enthusiasm far more convincingly than words can, but as we have learnt, our hands aren't always sending the right message. If you know that you talk with your hands, recognise that what you 'say' is not always what is 'heard' and that for many people, passion is not appropriate in a place of business.

Are there any other things to consider in light of what you've learnt from this chapter?

_____

_____

_____

_____

_____

References

- http://www.dailymail.co.uk/travel/travel_news/article-3000521/Handy-infographic-explains-hand-gestures-world.html

- http://www.healthytravelblog.com/2012/07/31/travel-etiquette-part-2-what-your-body-language-is-saying/

- Malcolm Gladwell, *Blink,* Penguin, London, 2005

- www.artofmanliness.com

4

'But I thought you Said...' Communication Differences

As children, we used to play a game called *Chinese Whispers,* also known as *Russian Scandal*. It involved whispering a sentence into somebody's ear, that person then passed it on to the next person, and on it went around a circle until at the end, something completely unrelated would be heard. A famous but apocryphal example in war-time Britain was 'Send reinforcements we're going to advance' being misheard as 'Send three and fourpence, we're going to a dance.' Working across cultures, with or without the added complexity of a second language, can be much like a game of Chinese Whispers in that what you *say* is often quite different to what is *heard*.

A few years ago, I was asked to help a French client with what he called their 'rude American client'. The teleconferences that the two held were a constant source of conflict. The French found the Americans a bit too hasty to get started; only interested in exchanging a few pleasantries and then getting down to business. They also felt the Americans were not interested in really having a proper discussion, they just wanted a decision or an action plan without actually exploring all the options. When I heard the French describe how brusque their clients were, I too was shocked, but when I actually sat in on a teleconference, it was obvious to me that the issues were much more to do with having different approaches than lack of manners.

The Americans were simply doing things their way – a bit of small talk, outcome focused, a 'time is money' attitude – and the French wanted to do it their way – spending time deepening the relationship and enjoying the intellectual rigour of a well-structured argument. As an English speaker, I would not personally have been offended by the American approach, but being a French speaker too, I could see how their directness and lack of 'politesse' could be interpreted as abrasive. As always, a little research and a little effort would have greatly helped each party to communicate more effectively.

A German colleague of mine, Miriam, recounted her experience of having a public argument with another German colleague while they were both working in Australia:

Both young women, Miriam and Renata disagreed strongly about an issue and both vociferously argued their case in the weekly team meeting. After the meeting, their Australian manager took them aside;

'That was pretty awkward for everyone,' he said. 'I get that you disagree and that you don't particularly like each other, but you have to keep your personal feelings out of the workplace ok? I'll split you up as much as I can, but you have to try and get along with each other.'

Miriam said that she and Renata had looked at each other and burst out laughing. They had in fact been on their way out to lunch – together – when he stopped them and they were completely taken aback by his reaction. In Germany, professional opinions will rarely impact on personal relationships and mounting an intelligent, structured argument against your colleague is perfectly acceptable – he or she may even compliment you on your argument, while at the same time disagreeing with you. In Australia, however, individuals are often reluctant to speak in a way that suggests they think they are intellectually superior. It is more common to downplay their intelligence and to use a simpler word instead of a more complex one, for fear that somebody might think they have too high an opinion of themselves. This sense of modesty is referred to as the 'Tall Poppy Syndrome'.

Even if the *words* of the presentation or meeting are in our own language, what you *say* is not always what is *heard*, and similarly, what you *hear* is not always what was *said*. There are many other verbal communication blunders that you can make, aside from those using language. Before you address those, however, let's take a moment to consider how challenging work can be for those people doing everything that you are doing – but in a language not their own.

> Even if the *words* of the presentation or meeting are in our own language, what you *say* is not always what is *heard*...

More ESL Issues

English is clearly the dominant business language of the world and those of us fortunate enough to have been born into English-speaking families should thank our lucky stars every day. There are many potential stumbling blocks in cross-cultural communication – business or otherwise – but none so consistently trips people up as when only one party is working in their own language.

A frequent complaint about video and teleconferences is that some people just don't say anything. Funnily enough, this is often the people with ESL issues, who are so busy keeping up with what is being said, that they can only follow the discussion but cannot really contribute to it. Some people are even doing their own simultaneous translation. If suddenly someone asks 'Hey Ming, what do you think we should do about this?', how likely is it that Ming will be able to come up with a convincing response?

A colleague of mine was in Tokyo recently for a three-day regional meeting and described the meeting to me on his return. In the group were four Americans, two English people and about fifteen Japanese. This was an internal meeting, for discussing business growth and strategy and for building team morale, but as he described it, it was anything but:

> 'The Americans just dominated the meeting', my English colleague told me. 'I found it really embarrassing, our colleagues from Japan literally could not get a word in between the fast-paced exchange and if they were asked a question and took more than a few seconds to answer it, the discussion just moved on without them. I kept thinking to myself that it was such a one-sided discussion, it was a waste of time including them and they must have thought we were incredibly arrogant.'

Accents can also pose problems, even if the person's level of English is very good. While working with a large French company, I delivered some cultural training to the teams both in France and in Australia and seemed to have ironed out a number of the wrinkles that were threatening to destabilise the teams. However, when one of the French team members was in Australia recently, I asked her how the latest team meeting had gone. Apparently it had not been very worthwhile for most of the French team, because the person doing most of the talking for the Australian team had a thick Irish accent which, when combined with the problems we discussed in Chapter 2 – including speed, interruptions and use of slang and jargon – made it virtually impossible for any of them to understand much of what was discussed. One of the biggest complaints about call centres similarly, is not that the consultants lack knowledge, but that their advice can be difficult to understand because of their accents.

The speed of conversation and how many people are taking part in a conversation impacts greatly on comprehension. Many ESL speakers can understand English perfectly when listening to one well-spoken person, such as an English teacher or a radio presenter, but when people are in groups they tend to speed up, interrupt each other and sometimes talk over each other, making it much harder. As my English colleague found in the story told above, needing to think on their feet in order to participate in a fast-flowing conversation also puts huge pressure on people.

But We Both Speak English...

In cross-cultural situations it is often mistakenly assumed that if two people are speaking the same language, there will be no cultural differences. Clearly this is not the case, as language is not culture, it's merely a means of communicating. George Bernard Shaw described America and England as "two countries divided by a common language" and that is just as true now as it was 150 years ago – in fact probably more so. So although perhaps not as common, mistakes and misunderstandings do frequently occur between people who speak the same language and would view themselves as similar.

America and Australia are on the surface so similar, but scratch the surface and there are many differences. Despite a notionally flat management structure, there is an underlying hierarchy in America which is evident in the use of titles, qualifications and forms of address. The autonomy and independence enjoyed in Australia is more unusual in America and the casual, often jokey references to sexual orientation, race and religion which are lightly bandied about in the Australian workplace often shock employees from the more litigious USA. Similarly, the enthusiastic self-promotion and the determined focus on quarterly results and signing up the next customer, is often felt to be too transactional by the relationship oriented and more laid-back Australians, where small talk is an important element of any meeting and 'catching up for a coffee' is seen as a great way to build relationships.

Likewise, despite its appearance as a very Anglo society – or indeed perhaps because of the expectation that Australia is just another English county, but with more sunshine – expatriates from the UK can also struggle in Australia. They don't expect Australia to be so different; for people to be quite so direct, for social codes to be quite so relaxed, for Australians to be quite so hard to make friends with and for the "no worries" culture to be quite so pervasive.

The simple phrase "we should have a beer sometime" is a good example of the different approaches. In America the invitation will be offered readily and expected to be taken up; in Australia the phrase is offered constantly and rarely expected to be taken seriously and in Britain it is not used at all until it is certain that having a beer would be a good idea for all concerned!

When moving from an English speaking country to say China or Russia, people expect life to be difficult. They mentally prepare for challenges in the workplace and for issues on the home front and, if and when problems do arise, they are not necessarily any easier to deal with, but at least they are ready for them. Moving to another English speaking country in many ways lulls people into a fall sense of security; they confuse language with culture and imagine that because they use the same words, the meaning conveyed will be the same too. Effective communication is of course about so much more than words and learning to read between the lines is an essential skill to acquire if expatriates are to succeed.

Silence is Golden

Even when you're not saying *anything*, you're saying something. In Asian societies and also in Australian Indigenous communities, questions are often met with silence and this 'thinking time' can go on for several minutes, during which time the thinker will look down or away. This can feel very awkward for Westerners, who tend to be much more comfortable with words than with silence. Silence to them indicates either a lack of understanding or an absence of conviction.

If you are a 'talker', it is essential that you become more comfortable with silence, as you can often talk yourself *out* of a deal. A Korean or Thai businessperson quietly musing to himself about the great deal in front of him will often be interrupted by his Western colleague, offering him further incentives, which are actually not necessary to complete the deal.

> If you are a 'talker', it is essential that you become more comfortable with silence, as you can often talk yourself *out* of a deal.

My friend Michael, who worked in Japan for several years, says he greeted all the new expatriates with a pen and a notebook and the instructions 'When the client starts thinking, you start writing.

I don't care what you write, a letter to your mother or a shopping list, just don't break the silence!'

Why Use Ten Words When One Will Do?

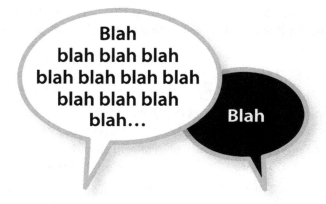

Even relative silence is generally a pretty uncomfortable concept for many Westerners. It's accepted that couples or friends who have known each other a long time can be happy in a 'companionable silence' but in other situations, silence does not indicate consent or agreement. On the contrary, silence is often assumed to mean that one party is not happy and of course that can be worrying.

A few years ago I bumped into my friend Isabel, as we were both heading into work on the train. As her station approached she mentioned that she was on her way to meet a potential client, a Finnish man.

'What are your chances?' I asked her.

'I've got no idea,' she said. 'He's a funny guy, he hardly says a word, I don't even know why he wants to meet us really.'

'Oh that tends to be just the Finnish way,' I said. 'They often prefer not to use ten words when one will do. Don't worry about it!'

Isabel rang me later to say that they had indeed got the job and that for her, just knowing that the Finns were often less than chatty, allowed her not to worry about it in their meeting. While her colleague was convinced that they hadn't impressed the client, because the Finn made hardly any comments, Isabel was able to relax with the relative silence and didn't try to force the man into conversation.

Other cultures where it's generally preferable to talk less rather than more include Austria, Belgium, Japan, the Czech Republic and Iceland. Iceland even has a social media site dedicated to silence, while conversely the five most talkative countries are USA, India, Canada, Nigeria and the UK.

Not Funny Anymore

Unless you are very familiar with your audience, telling a joke at the beginning of your presentation or meeting is potentially one of the worst things that you can do. Many Westerners – including the British, Americans, Australians and some Northern Europeans – like to start a talk with an anecdote or joke, designed to make their audience relax and to create a bit of warmth. In Germany and many South East Asian countries, however, humour has little place in business and may give the impression that the meeting is not really serious or important to you.

In meetings where another language is being spoken, and possibly a translator is being used, the potential to backfire is even greater as the concept of the joke literally may not translate, so the speaker is left with an embarrassingly big smile on their face and a lot of blank looks on those of their audience. Remember too that many jokes are told at the expense of others and in more collective cultures (see next chapter), this is strictly no-go. Although it certainly happens in private, saying something derogatory about someone else in public is frowned upon and may make the audience worry about what could be said about *them* in the next meeting. The type of jokes that are typically made in many Western meeting rooms – especially internal meetings – likewise need to be approached with caution; teasing Thai or Japanese colleagues about being a little late to a meeting could cause them embarrassment and loss of 'face'.

Face

'Face' is a concept that anyone wishing to do business in Asia or the Middle East needs to understand and master. Face equates to something like personal pride but it also has to do with public standing. Not only do people expect to be treated with respect, but they may also hope to boost their own reputation and status by being associated with you and your company. Their reputations are therefore somewhat in *your* hands. If you behave badly, they go down with you, hence the preference for building a relationship slowly and being quite certain of your calibre before they go into partnership with you.(See Chapter 9).

Face can be thought of as a commodity that can be traded; it can be given as a gift or taken away as a punishment. But just like a real gift, the act of exchanging face affects both the giver and the receiver. If you pay someone a compliment in front of other team or meeting members – for example saying 'Thanks Jung, that was really great work on the spreadsheet' – you not only give Jung positive face, but you also *earn* face by being a supportive manager. Unfortunately, the reverse also applies and if you are overly critical of someone, or rude, they lose face by being shamed and you lose face for your insensitivity.

Also important to remember is that, with face, a trade of equal if not greater value is expected. If your Malaysian or Jordanian client toasts you at a dinner and says how fortunate he feels to be working with you, the expected response is not that you just smile modestly, but that you raise a toast in response saying that indeed, the privilege is all yours, as clearly he is an important man in the business community. In nearly all cultures a better outcome is received if any wrongdoing or any type of sensitive issue is dealt with privately rather than publicly, but in cultures where face is so important, causing someone to lose face in public can lead to permanent damage to a relationship.

Face can be affected both by your own actions and by the actions of others. If you turn up to a meeting in Japan and they have a gift for you, but you don't have one for them, you lose face. If your Indian clients take you out for a dinner while you are in Bangalore, but when they visit Los Angeles you don't return the hospitality, you lose face. On the other hand, if during the lead-up to the mid-Autumn Zhong Qui Jie festival you turn up to your Beijing office not just bearing a box of Moon Cakes but also having done a little research into what the celebration is all about, your personal face ratings will soar! Note that the value of the gifts

> If your Indian clients take you out for a dinner while you are in Bangalore but when they visit Los Angeles you don't return the hospitality, you lose face.

exchanged should be similar, so that one party is not shamed by looking cheap. In cultures where gift giving is normal procedure (as opposed to Western cultures, which typically only adopt the practice to fit in), gifts are never opened in front of the giver, precisely to avoid such potential embarrassment.

Face is contagious and if your colleague does something shameful, you may also be brought into disrepute, as these stories illustrate;

In Korea a few years ago, an employee who sold information to a competitor was the source of great shame for everyone who worked for that company, as though they themselves had committed the crime.

In Sydney, a fifteen-year-old Chinese girl got very drunk at a party and had to be collected by her parents. Apparently a very pretty girl, she had beautiful long hair which she was very proud of. However, her parents were so deeply ashamed of her actions and the bad light that they felt had been cast on them, that she was not only grounded, but further punished by having all her hair cut off.

In countries like Korea and Japan, genuine remorse must be expressed if the person is to have any chance of having his or her face restored.

Marcia was a young American student on exchange in Kyoto, who inadvertently stole a bicycle and was subsequently arrested. At the police station, she explained how this had occurred – it can be confusing, there are so many bikes and so few of them are locked – and she apologised, but that was not enough. Before they would release her, she had to cry and show genuine remorse for having distressed the owner of the bicycle.

Small Talk, Big Impact

Making small talk is a big deal for some people. And while some people are very good at making small talk in their own country or culture, they can bomb horribly in another culture – confusingly, for precisely the same reasons that they are a success in their own.

Being able to make and *enjoy* small talk is seen as critical to success in many business environments and the topics are not always small either. While the conversation may start with general pleasantries about the weather and traffic, it can soon lead on to weightier topics such as literature, history and global issues and each person is expected to be able to contribute to this discussion. Whereas in many (not all) Western cultures, small talk is literally a 'small' conversation held before the main event, in non-Western cultures it *is* the main event. In the USA, for example, small talk is primarily seen as a precursor to the sales process, but in India and in France – among other countries – small talk is the basis of relationship-building and being too quick to get to your pitch will be frowned upon, at least during the first few meetings.

> Being able to make and *enjoy* small talk is seen as critical to success in many business environments and the topics are not always small either.

Many Westerners may consider that their family and their personal life are not really topics for discussion, but in a lot of African, South American, Asian and Southern European countries, this is precisely what people will want to talk about, as Anne found out:

> *Anne was a senior HR manager and was transferred from Adelaide to Mumbai for two years.*

'I can't get over the level of personal enquiry and personal disclosure that goes on here!' She wrote to me after a month or so. 'I know you told me I had to be prepared to ask all the questions which I was expressly forbidden to ask in Australia, but I really didn't believe people would also be asking me why I'm thirty years old and not married yet!'

We all like to think that we have a unique offering, but the reality is that many of the services we offer can be provided just as well by a dozen other people. What, then, would make someone choose you and your company? We discussed rapport in Chapter 2 and feeling that you are on the same 'cultural wavelength' with someone is a very big part of this. The Vietnamese, for example, love poetry and literature and expressing even a vague familiarity with this will earn you lots of credit. If people ask you about your family, it is because they are genuinely interested and hope that by sharing this personal information, your relationship will deepen. It would be insulting to them if you did not make similar enquiries of their family or refused an invitation to join them at a family celebration such as a wedding.

Conversational Style

Our comfort with small talk and skill in making it is, of course, hugely impacted by our cultural style. Many Southern Europeans and South Americans are renowned for the passion with which they express their views and both meetings and mealtimes can be noisy affairs. Hand gestures are common, as are raised voices and emotive exhortations and these can all be quite confronting to people from 'quieter' cultures.

A Greek friend of mine recounts a story of travelling in Greece and seeing a young Swedish woman trying to buy a ferry ticket. In struggling to understand each other, the Greek man got louder and louder, waving his arms about and thumping the desk, while the

young girl got more and more anxious and eventually burst into tears.
At this point the Greek man rushed around the desk and clasped her
by the arms.

'I'm not angry!' he shouted at her. 'I'M JUST GREEK!'

In more individualistic countries such as the USA and Australia, people are encouraged to be self-confident and assertive. Younger people will converse as equals with older or more senior people, they are happy to offer information about themselves and are not afraid to promote themselves to some extent. If they feel that someone can be of help to them, they may ask outright for support, asking them for an introduction for example, or to read something they have written. They will happily speak more loudly if the environment requires it and the conversation will likely be fast moving and generally upbeat.

In more collective and usually more hierarchical cultures, like sub-Saharan African countries and much of Asia, people tend to be more reluctant to draw attention to themselves as individuals. They would certainly not see themselves as able to converse on equal terms with older or more senior people and typically will be more modest about their achievements. Although perhaps very outgoing in their private lives – people in Sub-Saharan Africa, for example, will happily joining in with group activities such as spontaneous outbreaks of dancing in the street and so on – it is not seen as appropriate for anyone other than a fairly senior figure to be overly assertive or to make themselves the centre of the conversation. Many younger Asian managers coming to work in Australia really struggle with going to networking events; they hate the idea of having to walk up to a complete stranger, introduce themselves and start talking business with someone who may turn out to be considerably senior to them.

Richard D Lewis, author of *When Cultures Collide* and founder of Richard Lewis Communications, describes a number of different communication styles in his book which are well worth looking at. The styles are shown as illustrations, but are paraphrased in *Business Insider* magazine (using some of Lewis' words) as things like:

> *[The] English tend to avoid confrontation in an understated, mannered, and humorous style that can be both inefficient and powerful ... French tend to engage vigorously in a logical debate ... Spanish and Italians 'regard their languages as instruments of eloquence and they will go up and down the scale at will, pulling out every stop if need be to achieve greater expressiveness.'*

> *Scandinavians often have entrenched opinions that they have formulated 'in the long dark nights,' while the Swiss tend to be straightforward and unaggressive negotiators, who obtain concessions by expressing confidence in the quality and value of their goods and services.*

> *Indian English 'excels in ambiguity, and such things as truth and appearances are often subject to negotiation.' Australians tend to have a loose and frank conversational style ... Koreans tend to be energetic conversationalists who seek to close deals quickly, occasionally stretching the truth.*

Saying Yes, Meaning No

Many people from India, South East Asia and the Middle East have a reputation in the West for 'saying yes, but meaning no', as though they are deliberately setting out to trick Westerners with word games and duplicity. Much of this, however, is based on their desire to maintain harmony (a key tenet of Confucianism) and to not offend with a downright 'No'. It is considered extremely rude in these cultures to criticise someone publicly – especially a guest – and a refusal of your idea or suggestion would be just that.

In their minds, by using conditional phrases such as 'We would like to do that, *but* that will be quite difficult' or 'It's a great idea, *but* that might take a long time', they are making it quite clear that the answer is 'No'. The 'no' will almost certainly be indicated through

> **Many people from India, South East Asia and the Middle East have a reputation in the West for 'saying yes, but meaning no'...**

gestures and body language too, such as downcast eyes, slumped shoulders, an apologetic smile and so on. But because Westerners prefer a more direct form of communication, with black and white being the preferred colours and shades of grey just confusing, you can often struggle to interpret what you hear.

> *Many years ago in Nepal, I went out into the jungle on the back of an elephant, hoping to see a tiger. At several places, our guide would point to broken branches or to paw prints in the mud. At one point he crouched down over a pile of poo and announced 'This is a tiger who has been eating rabbit'. How on earth did he know? we wondered. The rabbit fur in the droppings were a dead giveaway, but only if you thought to look for it; to the rest of us – focussed solely on seeing a big striped cat – there was 'nothing to see'.*

In many ways, having a conversation with someone who either doesn't use many words, or constructs their sentences in a different way, can leave us feeling that nothing much has been said. Like the tracker, however, you just need to get more adept at looking for other signs, as you can be so busy looking for a tiger that you fail to see all the signs that will lead you to him. If you are in another country to sell your products and are only listening for a straight yes or no answer, you may get your hopes up in error and may also miss other opportunities which are being offered.

Grammatical differences can sometimes create problems in understanding. In most English speaking countries, for example, if I ask at my hotel 'Did anyone leave a parcel for me?' the concierge will reply 'No, nobody left a parcel for you'. In many Asian countries, however, the reply may well be 'Yes, nobody left a parcel' – meaning literally, 'Yes it's true, nobody left a parcel for you'. Asian people focus more on the auxiliary verb, whereas Westerners focus on the object. So if you ask 'Don't we have a meeting?', Asian people focus on the 'don't' and answer 'yes', which means 'I agree with what you say – we don't have a meeting'. 'Yes' also gets people into trouble when they assume that 'yes' means 'yes I agree' or even 'yes I want to buy it', rather than just 'Yes, I'm with you so far'. Confused?!

High & Low Context

The world can very loosely be divided into 'high context' and 'low context' cultures, a term coined by anthropologist Edward T Hall in 1976 in his book *Beyond Culture* and used as a broad definition of how cultural differences play out in different societies. Individuals can be both high and low context 'people' and situations within the same country can also be either, depending on what the situation is, but cultures often have a preference or bias for one style or the other.

'High context' refers to groups of people who know each other well, usually after spending a lot of time together. In a business context, a team who has worked together for several years has communal information that everyone knows and a stranger joining that group might find it difficult to join in. People from high context cultures regard what is *not* said – the French call it the *non-dit* or 'not-said' – as being just as important as what *is* said. Brazilians, Indians, Japanese, French, Hungarians and residents of many African countries rely on knowledge that comes from being a part of the group to explain something; the history or previous experience provides the context, not the words. In these high context cultures, words are just one means of communication. Of equal, if not greater importance, is the way that the words are spoken, the relationship of the speakers, what went on between them prior to this conversation, what else was spoken about at the time and even the actual time and place in which the discussion takes place.

A French client who became a friend moved to Japan as CEO of a multinational corporation (MNC). We went to stay with him after he had been there for a year and I asked him what had been his greatest difficulty in adapting to the Japanese culture. He thought for a while (clearly he had learned about active listening already) then replied:

'I've had to stop thinking out loud. If I muse about something, wondering for example what might be the impact on sales if we got a local celebrity to endorse our product, within a week I will have a 20-page report on my desk weighing up the pros and cons. There is an extraordinary willingness to be of service and just a hint is always enough to get something done. If the office is looking a bit untidy, for example, the department manager just has to suggest that if someone very important were to walk in, they wouldn't be very impressed and everyone rushes to tidy the place up. The problem for me is that I am still getting used to this level of responsiveness!'

In a social setting, if you have ever been to a party where everyone knows everyone else already, all live nearby, have children at the same schools and so on, you have been part of a high context group. An assumption is made that everyone in the group has similar understanding and knowledge; if guests are asked to 'bring a bottle' there is no need to specify that this should be wine, rather than fermented mare's milk. The playlist will consist of music that is well known to everyone and has everyone singing along with it and if the dress code is written as 'Black Tie', everyone knows that this doesn't mean a lounge suit with a black tie. (A common misunderstanding in Australia occurs when people are asked to 'Bring a Plate' to a party; this is shorthand for 'bring a plate of food to share with others' but many newcomers to Australia have just turned up with an empty plate, believing they would be taking some left-overs home with them.)

Not surprisingly, people from 'low context' cultures tend to be quite the opposite. Low context cultures include The Netherlands, Finland, Switzerland, Australia and the USA and people from these cultures tend to spell out all the details in words, leaving little to guesswork or assumption. Words outweigh every other tool of communication and they come thick and fast, with little time for reflection and with the assumption that if somebody has a question, they will ask it. Low context people have many relationships, but fewer deeper ones; 'time is money' and they tend to prefer not to invest too much of their time in developing a long-term relationship. They get down to business quickly, with just a little small-talk and are individuals rather than group-thinkers.

Western style business networking events tend to be very low context; attendees want to meet as many people as they can while they are there and to tell them about themselves and their product or service. Encounters are quickly summed up as 'useful' or 'not useful' and people move on. The notion of 'speed networking' would be perplexing indeed to people from high-context cultures! Other networking events can be both low and high-context; a get together of certified chartered accountants, for example, provides a high-context setting with much mutual knowledge, but the actual networking is likely to take place in a low-context style.

Email Etiquette

Emails can be a minefield when writing and reading them in your *own* language, add to that both language difficulties and cultural differences and not surprisingly, plenty of people end up being 'blown up'.

Below is a list of the most common mistakes that seem to occur regularly, most of which have as their root cause the fact that people do not respond *in kind*. For example;

• Person A writes a friendly, chatty email to person B – perhaps four or five lines long, saying how much they are looking forward to working with them and so on and ending up with offering a choice of dates on which they might meet. Person B responds with 'July 5'.

• Person A addresses the recipient by name and finishes with a personal sign off of some kind, such as Cheers or Kind regards. Person B doesn't use A's name in response or a friendly sign off, just jumps straight into the issue and signs off with their embedded signature.

• Person A begins their email with some personal niceties, such as 'hope all is well with you?', 'how was your trip to France?' and so on. Person B doesn't reply to these, or make similar enquiries of their own.

• Person A takes the trouble to write a long, explanatory email, Person B replies with 'OK'

• Person A is in one time zone and Person B is in another, yet 'A' expects a reply within their time frame and may even proceed with some point on the basis that "I didn't hear back from you on this, so assumed you were OK with it". (This happens frequently with one client of mine)

Of course, after exchanging several emails on a topic it's fine to dispense with the niceties and just answer the question, but initially it is courteous to answer in the same mode as Person A, or to take the time to start the exchange with a little warmth.

A few months ago I was exchanging emails with an Indian man who had spent the last ten years in Silicon Valley. I wrote to introduce myself prior to our cross cultural training session and made a point of welcoming him, saying that I was available beforehand if he or his wife had any questions, that I would happily go to his house to deliver the training and offering him a selection of dates. He replied 'March 3'.

Even as someone who *knows* that what you see is rarely what you get, it didn't make me feel very friendly towards him or to look forward to meeting him particularly, although he was in fact charming in person. Perhaps not surprisingly, one of the things I was asked to address by his CEO was his email and phone manner, as his brevity was creating difficulties for a number of his colleagues too.

Applying the Four R's

As if getting through 'the first five minutes' wasn't enough, in this chapter we have started to explore some of the verbal communication differences which can make communicating across cultures such a potential minefield as the meeting progresses. Remember that this book is not intended to make you self-conscious, but to make you self-aware. We all have spinach in our teeth from time to time, and perhaps after reading this chapter, you know exactly when that was. The thought of that joke you started your speech with, or that Japanese client who you kept badgering with questions, may now make you blush. Those issues will hopefully not occur again if you take the learnings from this chapter on board.

How would you apply the **Four R's** to these issues?

Rewards

Questions: Can you imagine ever feeling almost as comfortable working in another culture as you do in your own?

Considerations: We all want to be able to communicate, yet frequently our encounters with people from other cultures are a source of utter frustration. Maybe a warm lead has gone stone cold on you, the intern you had such high hopes of doesn't seem to be very engaged anymore or the expatriate assignment you were hoping for doesn't look very likely since your visit to head office in Tokyo. Things that would be more straightforward in your own culture seem so much harder in someone else's. How rewarding would it be to know why these things happened, instead of feeling disadvantaged by cultural nuances which you knew nothing about?

Research

Questions: Reading through these examples, are you reminded of times in your working life when you didn't feel fully prepared? Can you think of situations which you might try a different approach with now?

Considerations: Learning even a little about the importance of 'face' may make you change the way you manage your Chinese team. Understanding how to frame your questions so that they cannot be answered with a yes or a no may mean the end of the 'saying yes, meaning no' scenario which frustrates you so much. And who knew how reading about what makes Thai people proud could boost your small-talk capabilities, especially when combined with showing off your active listening skills?

Reflect

Questions: Did any of the points in this chapter make you feel just a little bit embarrassed as you remembered something you had done?

Considerations: Perhaps sometimes you force people to talk, because you are uncomfortable with silence yourself. Maybe you are overly impatient and interrupt people who are having trouble putting their thoughts into words, or you tease people if they get something wrong. Perhaps you have a natural tendency to talk about sport to your predominantly male colleagues, even though you know that some people clearly feel excluded by this. Be aware of why you do these things and the potential they have for creating negative outcomes.

Reach Out

Questions: What could you be doing more of, if you are
                  serious about creating better relationships?

Considerations: Put yourself in your colleague or your client's
                  shoes; how would you manage in their
                  situation? Can you be more supportive of their
                  concern not to lose face and difficulties with
                  making small talk? Perhaps you can become
                  more adept at listening for more than words;
                  try using your Inner Sherlock to uncover the
                  more indirect ways in which your client or
                  colleague is communicating, this will develop
                  your sensory acuity and help you to have
                  more realistic expectations of this relationship.
                  Your colleagues who have ESL issues might
                  enjoy greater support from you too, through
                  simple kindnesses such as avoiding jargon and
                  slowing your speech down.

Are there any other things to consider in light of what you've
learnt from this chapter?

_____

_____

_____

_____

_____

References

- Richard D Lewis, *When Cultures Collide,* Brealey, London, 1996 (Revised 2006) as quoted in http://www.businessinsider.com.au/communication-charts-around-the-world-2014-3

- Edward T Hall, *Beyond Culture*, Anchor Books, 1977

5

Ant or Colony?
Individualist & Collective
Societies

Defining people as either Individual or Collective was one of the first distinctions that cross-culturalists came up with. Both anthropologist Edward T Hall in 1976 and social psychologist and cross-culturalist Geert Hofstede in the 1980s included this aspect in the models they created to organise and to some extent predict behaviour across a range of different cultures. Hofstede described the Individualism versus Collectivism (IDV) dimension like this:

> *The high side of this dimension, called individualism, can be defined as a preference for a loosely-knit social framework in which individuals are expected to take care of only themselves and their immediate families. Its opposite, collectivism, represents a preference for a tightly-knit framework in society in which individuals can expect their relatives or members of a particular in-group to look after them in exchange*

for unquestioning loyalty. A society's position on this dimension is reflected in whether people's self-image is defined in terms of 'I' or 'we.'

In his book *Global Dexterity*, Andy Molinsky takes a new approach to the idea of cultural dimensions and suggests instead that people need to have a 'cultural code' which helps them to determine the appropriate behaviour in a range of cross cultural situations. Interestingly, the six dimensions that he describes (see below) are *all impacted* by whether people think of themselves as an individual or as one of a collective:

- Directness: How straightforwardly am I expected to communicate in this situation?

- Enthusiasm: How much positive emotion and energy am I expected to show to others in this situation?

- Formality: How much deference and respect am I expected to demonstrate in this situation?

- Assertiveness: How strongly am I expected to express my voice in this situation?

- Self-promotion: How positively am I expected to speak about my skills and accomplishments in this situation?

- Personal disclosure: How much can I reveal about myself in this situation?

The idea of a 'collective' can embrace all types of groupings; tribal, caste, family, religious, organisational, gender, age and of course many more. But try these dimensions out, by applying them to people you know and you will find that there is a strong consistency in behaviour. In my opinion, if people identify with a group first, they are much more mindful of the impact of what they say or do on the group and will therefore tend to be:

- Less direct: 'It's not appropriate for me to force my view on the group.'

- Less enthusiastic: 'I don't want to enthuse too much until I know what everyone else thinks.'

- More formal: 'I will never get into trouble for being too polite.'

- Less assertive: 'It's not just what I want, I must accept what is best for the group.'

- Less likely to self-promote: 'It disrupts the harmony of the group to single myself out.'

- Less likely to self-disclose: 'I don't want to say what I think, in case it makes someone else feel bad.'

This reluctance to upset the collective apple cart can have huge knock-on effects, from people being reluctant to report a wrongdoing, being closed to outside influences, having to offer preferential treatment and rates to family and friends and much more. Gurnek Bains, in *Cultural DNA*, notes that in many African organisations, departments and teams form a very tight collective and it can be very hard to move people between departments. People also have a strong link to their

> This reluctance to upset the collective apple cart can have huge knock-on effects, from people being reluctant to report a wrongdoing, being closed to outside influences, having to offer preferential treatment and rates to family and friends and much more.

community or sometimes birthplace and find that they are not easily accepted outside of it, so moving a successful manager to another country or even another town can be very challenging.

Individualism also has its drawbacks of course. In *Expand Your Borders,* David Livermore writes that 'the Anglo cultures are largely organised around the idea of individual rights, freedom and responsibility ... [it] does not have, nor does it want, much emphasis on group loyalty and collective interest. The priority is most definitely upon individual goals and interest'. Ironically, for all that self-interest, our society of individuals is not necessarily a happy one.

All for One and One for All

Japan is one of the most collective societies on earth and in Osaka, Madoka had been on a production line assembling televisions for the last five weeks. Her colleagues had made her welcome and the factory floor manager, Takeshi-San, had taken care to ensure she knew what she needed to do. When the red light flashed to show that the assembly line had been halted due to a problem, her first thoughts were how ashamed she would be if it turned out to be her fault and how guilty she would feel if she had caused trouble for her colleagues.

As it turned out, it *was* Madoka's fault – but not in the eyes of her Japanese colleagues. The American HR manager, Jim, was called in to assess the situation and asked whose fault it was. Everyone kept themselves busy. But as Madoka blushed hotly and wished for the ground to open beneath her, the American grew more insistent.

> '*I want a name,*' he said to Takeshi-San. '*We can't afford mistakes like this, it's a huge waste of money and time. Who did this?*'

Takeshi-San looked away awkwardly. What good could come of shaming poor Madoka, he thought to himself, embarrassed by the American's lack of empathy. Jim waited several minutes more, impatiently tapping his foot, until finally Takeshi-San smiled gently at him and said: 'The person who did this is probably deeply ashamed. It would be very hard to single her out, so blame all of us instead – we are a team here and it was probably our fault, not hers, that the mistake happened. Maybe we didn't give her enough help? But don't worry, we will all work hard together to make sure this doesn't happen again. This is the way in Japan.'

The stand-off continued for a while longer, but Takeshi would not budge and eventually the American had to retreat without a name. In a highly collective society, Jim should never have tried to single someone out or indeed to get one individual to speak out against another. As a result of his ignorance, he lost an incredible amount of face – both for trying to punish an individual in front of their colleagues and causing *them* great loss of face and also for trying to insist on doing things his way. After the incident he found it increasingly difficult to introduce the new HR agenda he had plans for.

Jim had still to grasp the most basic principle of working in a country not your own: if there is one of you and many millions of them, how likely is it that they are going to do it *your* way? This will only ever happen if you can persuade them that your way is better for them. In the meantime, pretending the cultural differences don't matter because you are the boss, or ignoring them and hoping they will go away, are not effective strategies.

> Pretending the cultural differences don't matter because you are the boss, or ignoring them and hoping they will go away, are not effective strategies.

Me or We?

As an American, Jim was used to a society that favours the interests of the individual over those of the group. America, Australia, Great Britain and The Netherlands are all societies where people are expected to stand on their own two feet, to look after themselves and to be able to work without too much direction or supervision. They also like competition and can enjoy winning without feeling bad for those who lost. This is not to suggest that people in individualistic cultures don't care about their colleagues or about the company they work for, of course they do, but their motivation is more about what works best for them as individuals, rather than what works best for everyone.

In individualistic cultures, people work in teams for practical reasons; because it is more convenient to do so and because it allows you to get results faster and deliver better client servicing, for example. In many (but not all) Asian and South American cultures, strength is found in numbers and security in being part of the crowd. There is also a very strong sense of caring for and looking after others in the group. Although the phrase 'to take one for the team' is American in origin, ironically it suits collective societies very well, as members of those societies are generally very willing to share both the responsibility for any mistakes and the rewards of any successes. Where members of individualist societies might revel in awards such as 'Employee of the Month', such singling out would be horribly embarrassing for most Koreans or Ecuadoreans – almost to the point of being shameful. They would worry not only that it set them apart from the group,

> Although the phrase 'to take one for the team' is American in origin, ironically it suits collective societies very well...

but also that their colleagues would feel underappreciated. Expatriate managers need to be very sure whether they are offering someone a prize or a punishment.

> *Imagine a car dealership, for example, in an Australian town. The sales team will have individual targets and a league table to see how they are faring against other individuals, as well as a competition between their showroom and other showrooms around the country. In Malaysia, a more muted version of this happens and salespeople will undercut each other in order to get the sale, but not as aggressively. However, this type of behaviour is very unlikely to happen in Japan. Japan is not only collective, it is also a society which values quality and beauty in all things. It would be seen as harmful to both the team and the brand to sell an item only on price, so the emphasis is far more on the quality of the relationship and the excellence of the product.*

As we have seen earlier, it is never safe to assume that the strategies which worked for you in another country will also be successful for you elsewhere. No matter how much of a success you were in your previous role, your skills worked because they suited that context and that culture. Change the context and your strategies need to change too.

Conversation Stoppers

Many Westerners like to grumble that their more collective-minded colleagues don't contribute to meetings very much, whether in virtual or face-to-face situations. We explored this from an ESL point-of-view in Chapter 4, but it is also hugely impacted by the collective natures of these colleagues. A British colleague, Alex, described how frustrated he had been while attending a get-together of all the South-East Asian executives:

'I swear my Asian colleagues hardly said a word for the whole time. We really did give them lots of chances, we kept asking them for input and for their thoughts, but honestly they would just agree with everything. They spent a lot of time thinking but didn't really come up with any game changers, we pretty much had to think everything!'

'Was the meeting entirely in English?' I asked him.

'Of course!' he said, 'None of us speak Thai or Japanese or anything, but their English is pretty good and they can follow what's going on.'

Alex clearly felt that poor English would be the only reason that someone wouldn't speak out and as his colleagues had 'pretty good' English, why then were they holding back? A more culturally intelligent person would have known that there was far more than language involved. Certainly it would have been both challenging and exhausting for the others to keep up with a fast-paced, probably quite noisy discussion in a foreign language, but just as important was recognising the restraints imposed by their collectivism. A reluctance to single themselves out, to speak on behalf of others without having consulted them first, to assume that *their* point-of-view was worth listening to – all of these actions would be viewed as far too individualistic.

Another issue which divided the group was that the Anglo participants clearly expected that when asked for their input, the non-Anglos would have ideas on the tips of their tongues and would respond straight away. When they failed to do this, it was assumed they had nothing to contribute and the conversation moved on without them. However, the requirements of the 'active listening' style which the Asians were comfortable with were to listen respectfully, with full attention, make sure that you have understood the question and then think carefully before replying. This not only shows that you have given the question due consideration, but also avoids the potential embarrassment of getting something wrong. The Anglo group did not give them time to do any of these things.

Naturally not all people from collective societies are 'shrinking violets'; those who have spent time studying or working overseas will often display a greater level of assertiveness, but it is nonetheless very common for people with a collective *heritage* to be more restrained than their Western counterparts.

> Naturally not all people from collective societies are 'shrinking violets'; those who have spent time studying or working overseas will often display a greater level of assertiveness...

The Pursuit of Harmony

Many aspects of collective behaviour derive from what I refer to as 'The Pursuit of Harmony' and it is helpful to look briefly at some of these through this lens. In much of Asia, being in harmony is seen as critical to the smooth running of organisations, families and societies. Harmony entails, among other things, being closely in touch with nature; the Japanese practice 'forest bathing' as a way to relieve stress and to maintain their connection with the living planet. Also critical is the acceptance of the cyclical nature of events, as seen in the Indian belief in reincarnation. Finally, harmony relies on believing in the importance of a counter-balance at all times; growth must be followed by a slowdown, for example and there are consequences for every action. The Yin & Yang symbol expresses this perfectly, as does the practice of Feng Shui (see Chapter 8), which seeks to balance the contradictory effects of wind and water.

Consider, for example, the story of Madoka and Jim. Madoka's manager Takeshi-San didn't want the harmony of the team – indicated by their good working relationship and concern for each other – to be damaged. Alex's Asian colleagues did not want to potentially embarrass a colleague by putting them 'on the spot'. People say yes when they really mean no, because harmony cannot be maintained if someone is overly direct or doesn't care about the other person's feelings. People worry about losing face or about causing someone else to lose 'face' and hate to be singled out from the crowd in case other people feel overlooked. All of these actions are motivated by the same desire – to maintain harmony.

The Chinese refer to their system of doing business only with their trusted network as *guanxi*. This is discussed further in Chapter 9, but is worth referring to here also, in the context of maintaining harmony. Consider the fact that if a non-Chinese person hopes to achieve anything in a business sense, they must have a Chinese partner to effectively sponsor and vouch for them. Although this is regarded by many as protectionism, in the context of maintaining harmony it makes perfect sense, as the inherent harmony of the group could be compromised by the introduction of an unknown quantity. If harmony is always to be maintained in the group, it becomes a lot harder to insult or cheat anyone, to have a disagreement that turns into a shouting match or an ugly competition between individuals vying for the top job. It would of course be naïve to think that none of these things ever happen, but remembering this driver may sometimes help you to understand your clients' behaviour, to curb your frustration and just gracefully accept an invitation to another banquet.

Concern for Others

Concern for others is a key element of maintaining harmony and like collectivism and individualism is not, of course, just seen in business contexts but is reflected in the daily rituals of the society. Compare, for example, the behaviour of passengers on a suburban commuter train in Australia and Japan. In Australia, a society of individuals, it is not uncommon for people to listen to music at volumes that can be heard by other passengers, to have conversations without lowering their voices (either to the person they are sitting with, or with someone on the end of the phone) and to sometimes be quite indiscreet about situations arising both at work and in their private lives. It is also not unusual to see people put their feet on the seats (even though it is prohibited) and to leave food wrappings and newspapers on the seats when they leave.

> In Japan, *everybody* reads and conversation is minimal; many Japanese businesses in fact prohibit their employees from talking about their work in public places...

In Japan, *everybody* reads and conversation is minimal; many Japanese businesses in fact prohibit their employees from talking about their work in public places, in order to reduce the risk of being overheard by the wrong person. Passengers are also very mindful of maintaining a quiet and clean space for their fellow passengers. On a visit there with my teenage daughter, we got separated and ended up at opposite ends of the carriage; not wanting to lose her, I called out 'Next stop Pippa!' only to be shushed by half a dozen people in the carriage. Perhaps not surprisingly, the original Sony Walkman was invented by Japanese audio engineer Nobutoshi Kihara, so that he could listen to opera on his frequent plane trips *without disturbing other passengers.*

It is also interesting to note some of the many rules around civic behaviour in various countries. Again in Japan, taking your shoes off at the door is considered 'normal' behavior and it is also expected that you put special plastic shoes *on* to use the bathrooms. Many a Westerner has been embarrassed for wearing the special 'loo shoes' into the dining room. In Germany, it is illegal to cut your grass or hang your laundry outside on a Sunday, or to tune your piano at midnight. (Tuning your piano at midnight *should* be illegal everywhere!) In Switzerland, quiet hours are enforced between 12 noon and 2 p.m. daily and also all day Sunday and you cannot take a shower or flush the loo after 10 p.m. if you live in a flat.

There are also many social customs which are not enforced by law, but which may cause you to feel like an outsider if you don't participate in them. An Italian friend describes his elderly parents as 'social Catholics':

> *'They don't really have faith any more, but their lives revolve around the church. If they stopped going to church on Sundays, they would have no social life either, as people would ostracise them. In that sense, they are locked in to the small mindset of a small town – they*

will have to go to church every Sunday for the rest of their lives, even though they would much rather be at home relaxing.'

As a woman in France, you may find you are the only woman in the bakery not wearing at least some lip gloss, as it is common practice there to make an effort for the people who have to look *at* you. French women have always been envied for their stylishness and a number of French women I have worked with have been shocked to see Australian women wearing their Ugg boots (sheepskin slippers) in the supermarket. They see it as a lowering of personal standards and disrespectful to your fellow shoppers not to make an effort.

> As a woman in France, you may find you are the only woman in the bakery not wearing at least some lip gloss, as it is common practice there to make an effort for the people who have to look *at* you.

On a more sombre note, the genocide in Rwanda in 1994 left many thousands of people with post-traumatic shock and many Western trained psychologists and health workers went to Rwanda to offer their help. What they offered was not popular, however, as the Western method of treatment was seen as adding even more pain to the sufferers. In his terrific TED talk *Depression: The Secret We Share*, writer Andrew Solomon recounts a conversation he had with a Rwandan man about this, who told him:

> *… we've had a lot of trouble with Western mental health workers, especially the ones who came right after the genocide … they would do this bizarre thing. They didn't take people out in the sunshine where you begin to feel better. They didn't include drumming or music to get people's blood going. They didn't involve the whole community. They didn't externalize the depression as an invasive spirit. Instead what*

> *they did was they took people one at a time into dingy little rooms and*
> *had them talk for an hour about bad things that had happened to*
> *them … We had to ask them to leave the country.*

In general, both pain and joy are both better experienced communally in most African countries, particularly sub-Saharan ones, and this is seen clearly in the popular African philosophy of *Ubuntu*. *Ubuntu* is all about the colony rather than the ant; indeed, the ant is only as strong as the colony that protects it. In a continent continually ravaged by extreme weather and tribal in-fighting, group strength is essential for survival and politicians frequently refer to *Ubuntu* as a reminder to people of the importance of unity. Archbishop Desmond Tutu describes *Ubuntu* like this:

> *A person with Ubuntu is welcoming, hospitable, warm and generous,*
> *willing to share. Such people are open and available to others, willing*
> *to be vulnerable, affirming of others, do not feel threatened that*
> *others are able and good, for they have a proper self-assurance that*
> *comes from knowing that they belong in a greater whole. They know*
> *that they are diminished when others are humiliated, diminished*
> *when others are oppressed, diminished when others are treated as if*
> *they were less than who they are. The quality of Ubuntu gives people*
> *resilience, enabling them to survive and emerge still human despite all*
> *efforts to dehumanize them.*

I remember watching, of all things, the film of *Lady Chatterley's Lover* whilst in Botswana. The audience were incredibly involved and every time the pathos or the tension built, the audience would shout out helpful advice to the actors about how to resolve their dilemma – much of it unprintable here! On buses and public taxis, I frequently found myself holding a baby or a chicken for someone who had too many packages to manage themselves and they never asked me, it was just assumed that people would help one another out. My inexperienced handling of travelling chickens was frequently cause for much hilarity among the passengers, but they were always friendly and also incredibly generous with sharing their food and even opening their homes to me.

Many migrants and refugees from Africa who end up in the northern hemisphere find not only the climate to be cold, but also struggle with isolation and loneliness. Buses on which nobody speaks to the person sitting next to them, shops in which nobody stops for a chat and streets where people don't even know their neighbours must seem chilly indeed.

Applying the Four R's

This chapter has explored the differences in the individual and the collective approaches that you may experience when working across cultures. As always, it is not that one approach is right and the other is wrong, more that they are very different operating systems – like diesel and petrol. Diesel fuel may deliver a great result in your diesel car, but not only will it not get you far in your petrol-powered one, it will also do considerable damage to your engine. This can end up costing a great deal of time and money to put right, much like a number of international mergers and acquisitions which have started so promisingly but ended so badly.

How would you apply the **Four R's** to this issue?

Rewards

Questions: Assuming that you are an individualist, how would you propose to reward someone who came from a collective society and how difficult might this be?

Considerations:	Once you understand that people in collective societies want to be seen to be contributing to the teams' progress, standing or well-being, you can ensure that your reward acknowledges the achievement and contribution of both the individual and the group. For example, give the individual a big box of cookies to share with her team rather than giving just her a bunch of flowers.

Research

Questions:	How could Jim have avoided losing face and causing shame to Madoka?
Considerations:	Clearly Jim had no idea how to manage the situation he found himself him. Ideally, of course, he would have learnt beforehand through cross cultural training or at least his own preparation, but failing that he could also have asked Takeshi-San how to resolve it. The challenge, however, was not just that Jim lacked the emotional intelligence required to read the situation, he also didn't know that he didn't know. Like many others we have met, he was not aware of having any gaps in his knowledge until suddenly a situation turned out very differently to how he expected.

Reflect

Questions:	Are you more naturally an individual or a collective type? Have you always been this way

or has your attitude changed since living in a different country?

Considerations: Although you may have been brought up to live one way, often experiencing another way of doing things can have a life-changing effect. People who repatriate after an overseas assignment often struggle with this; having learned to view the world through a different lens, they can find that they actually prefer it. Third-culture kids can also struggle with this, for example being encouraged to be assertive and independent at work, yet rewarded for being compliant and self-deprecating at home.

Reach Out

Questions: Effective communication between an individualist and a collectivist can be very hard to get right. People from individualistic cultures see asking people individually for their thoughts as giving them an opportunity to shine – this is what they would like for themselves! – and don't consider how going out on a limb could be worrying for some people. What strategies would help them to communicate?

Considerations: Alex, like Jim, gave no thought as to *why* his Asian colleagues didn't say much, he simply made an assumption based on his own values. He needed to ask, not assume and he also needed to become very competent at active listening, so as to give his colleagues the breathing space they needed without them feeling pressured by him. Supporting his colleagues with ESL would have been considerate and kind and would have earned him a great deal of face.

Are there any other things to consider in light of what you've learnt from this chapter?

_____

_____

_____

_____

_____

References

- Bishop Tutu as quoted on Buzzle: http://www.buzzle.com/editorials/7-22-2006-103206.asp

- https://geert-hofstede.com/national-culture.html

- Andrew Solomon, TED Talk *Depression: The Secret We Share*, www.ted.com, 2013

- Edward T Hall, *Beyond Culture*, Anchor Books, 1977

- David Livermore, *Expand Your Borders*, Cultural Intelligence Centre LLC, Michigan 2013, p22

- Gurnek Bains, *Cultural DNA*, Wiley, New Jersey, 2015 pp. XI

- Andy Molinsky, *Global Dexterity*, Harvard Business Review Press, Boston, 2013, p14

6

Wrong Direction Management & Motivation Differences

A few years ago I came across an American management book in a garage sale called *How to Motivate Your Slacking Team,* by Derek Hamilton. I was appalled that someone had purchased it, but heartened by the fact that they were now getting rid of it!

How to manage and motivate people is naturally what every expatriate seeks to understand. Some level of pushback and resistance is bound to be experienced – on both sides – but of course, being able to bring the team around is essential if the mission is to be fulfilled.

However, anyone wishing to communicate effectively with someone from another culture first of all needs to hold up a mirror and see themselves as others see them. This is much harder than it sounds, as we tend to have a blind spot when it comes to understanding how we may be perceived by others. Nearly all of us are certain that what we do is 'normal' and that it's everyone else who is different, but of course that is how *they* see it too. A fish has no concept of how happy it is swimming in water until suddenly it finds itself flapping on a bank and gasping for air. In many ways, travelling and especially working overseas can make a flailing fish out of all of us. Cross cultural author and researcher Andy Molinsky writes in an article in the *Harvard Business Review* of the need for leaders in cross cultural situations, or managers of cross cultural teams, to be adept at what he calls "cultural code switching". Also known as 'cultural fluency' or 'cultural agility', it refers to the ability to adjust your style to suit your employee or manager, in much the same way as when you visit another country, you may need to change your language or the side of the road on which you drive.

> One of the biggest difficulties for global employees is adapting themselves to the management style of the new country.

One of the biggest difficulties for global employees is adapting themselves to the management style of the new country. Of course, this is easy to say but much harder to do. People spend years learning how to behave in the particular way that suits their home culture and suddenly they are asked to unlearn it. If you break your arm and have to do everything from brushing your teeth to doing up buttons with the 'wrong hand', you begin to have some inkling of how challenging it can be.

This is equally challenging and equally important whether you are managing or being managed. Unfortunately, so few expatriates receive cross cultural training that many expatriates will start a new job with a mindset of 'this strategy worked for me at home in my last job, so I'll just keep doing it here'. What made you a successful CEO in France, however, does not guarantee you success in Australia, and what made you a great account executive in Hong Kong, may not win you any prizes in America.

You might find the following topics helpful to bear in mind.

Keep the Team Informed

One of the most common mistakes I encounter in my work is that new managers are so busy sorting themselves out, that they don't make any time to tell their team what their plans are. Of course, it's a really busy time and people are on a very steep learning curve, but engaging the team in the first week or two, *maximum*, is essential. They are all asking themselves and each other 'What about me? What's going to happen to us?' but often by the time they actually get told, distance has already been created and momentum has been lost. Add to this that the new manager may have a very different management style, may send quite terse sounding emails because his English is a bit limited, doesn't join the others for a drink on Friday night because his wife has been on her own all week and suddenly, everyone's feeling very nervous.

Take Jurgen, for example, who recently transferred to Sydney from Germany;

> *Jurgen is an engineer and he has been sent to Sydney to introduce various systems improvements. He is German and his predecessor was Swiss. To many Australians, this is the same thing; they expect both to fit the German stereotype of being overly serious, lacking a sense of humour and obsessed with formality and punctuality. His predecessor sacked half the team and now Jurgen has arrived talking about 'improvements' and 'greater efficiencies', words that inevitably make employees anxious.*

In fact, Jurgen is nothing like this, but he has not taken the time to demonstrate this to his team. He plans to host weekly breakfasts and bring in fresh pastries from a nearby German bakery, as he used to do at home and he plans to buy a ping-pong table for the cafeteria, but while he waits, the anxiety amongst his team grows and if he doesn't do it soon, the moment for enthusing them and getting them on board will be lost.

Iron or Putter?

Just as in golf there are different clubs to use, depending on whether you want to drive the ball down the fairway or nudge it into the hole, there are employees who will respond more positively to irons than putters. In other words, some employees will be confused by attempts to manage them that, to them, don't seem to make much sense or which they have no previous experience of.

> Just as in golf there are different clubs to use, depending on whether you want to drive the ball down the fairway or nudge it into the hole, there are employees who will respond more positively to irons than putters.

For example, many Indian businesses still have a very hierarchical, paternalistic structure, in which senior staff issue instructions and junior staff do what is asked. This is changing as more and more Indians attend Western business schools, but old habits die hard and when a Western-educated manager tries to encourage the team to come up with some ideas of their own, this is frequently met with confusion. 'Why are they asking me? They're the boss!' would be a common response.

In Australia, by contrast, many managers practice what could loosely be called a 'delegate and disappear' style of management. Australians are highly individualistic and like to be given the opportunity to work things out for themselves, to demonstrate their skills and prove that they don't need micro-managing. As in Nordic countries, in North America and Northern Europe, the team members' input is encouraged by their boss; if they disagree with him or her they are free to say so, provided they can back up their point of view. They are also welcome to expand on the boss's idea or to suggest modifications. But this kind of free exchange of ideas is not at all common in most Asian countries and consequently employees from those countries are often regarded as lacking in ideas and initiative, whereas in fact they simply need a lot more encouragement to speak out. They also need *time* in which to make this adjustment – often several months, at least.

> **Australians are highly individualistic and like to be given the opportunity to work things out for themselves, to demonstrate their skills and prove that they don't need micro-managing.**

Robert is from China and had this experience when he went to Melbourne about five years ago to join a financial services company;

In our first coaching session I asked Robert how he responded when his boss in China floated an idea that he felt unsure about? He just smiled and said 'I always tell him that it's a great idea'.

We spoke about the lack of hierarchy in Australia and the very open management style which encourages employees to participate, show initiative and come up with ideas themselves. How, due to the challenging nature of its early settlement, Australia has a 'frontier mentality' which recognises that not every expedition results in success, but it's essential to keep exploring. While of course failure is not seen as desirable, there is nonetheless a tolerance for failure and a view that it is a learning experience. As long as it was felt that someone had really done all that they could, it was accepted that sometimes, despite the best intentions, things just don't go according to plan.

We probably spent half an hour on this point and I then asked him, 'So, when your Australian boss suggests something that you're not sure will work, what do you think you will say?'

He just smiled and said 'I will just tell him it's a great idea'.

> **Unlike Australia, France has very little tolerance for failure and the buck stops definitively with the CEO.**

Unlike Australia, France has very little tolerance for failure and the buck stops definitively with the CEO. Any failure that occurs on their watch is their personal responsibility and can be very damaging to their career. French managers and executives, therefore, will go to great lengths to ensure they are across everything going on in their organisation – a management style that doesn't go down at all well in less-hierarchical cultures. Jean-Pierre was a French executive who took up a CEO role in Brisbane, with very poor outcomes:

Jean-Pierre was most comfortable being informed of all the details and being responsible for signing off on any actions by his executive team. His micro-management style took away responsibility and autonomy from senior executives, who were used to managing their own areas, causing frustration, resentment and considerable fear. They thought he was trying to get across their areas so he could make them redundant; he thought they were trying to hide things from him.

Within a few months, there were grumblings and then resignations, all because nobody had understood that the French and the Australians work on very different operating systems.

If it happens at all, cross cultural training is usually only undertaken by the newcomer and not by the person who will be managing them. This is usually justified by the argument that the newcomer has to assimilate and learn the local ways of doing things, which in so many ways negates the whole benefits of having a diversity of perspective – but that's another story. However this assimilation versus acculturation argument also doesn't take into account the fact that because people have different *learning styles*, they are used to different *teaching styles,* so instruction may very well fall on deaf ears, as Swee-Nor's manager found;

Swee-Nor was from Malaysia and worked for a large consultancy. She had not received any cultural training and her manager contacted me several months after her arrival, complaining that she just couldn't follow through on simple tasks he asked of her. It turned out that a frequent 'simple task' was to chase up clients for some documentation or figures which had been promised multiple times, but never actually delivered. Swee-Nor's job was effectively to keep chasing the client until they sent the information and she found this very challenging. As a young Malaysian woman, the idea of hounding someone who was both older, more senior, often a male and a client, was like asking her to walk on water. Too unsure of her ground and too nervous to explain her predicament to her manager, she resorted to telling him that she had made the follow-ups he requested and the information would be with them any day. Eventually of course, it all came unstuck.

After a number of similar incidents at both Robert and Swee-Nor's firms, training was arranged for their managers too, so that they understood the differences and could accommodate them. This was very successful but is unfortunately, fairly uncommon. As mentioned earlier, one of the biggest challenges is that people *don't know what they don't know*, so they cannot appreciate how much training would benefit them. When training *is* offered, it's almost always on an optional basis and those who would most benefit from it are inevitably the ones who lack the self-awareness to see how much they need it. Add to this that training usually has to take place at an exceptionally busy time for them and most people will opt out if they can.

'If You Are Leading and Nobody Is Following, You're Just Taking a Walk'

This Afghan proverb has been reworked many times, but it's meaning is always the same – if you don't inspire people, you are not a true leader. In different cultures, leaders are both treated differently and expected to behave differently, and one of the many challenges for global leaders and managers is that, like Jean-Pierre above, what constitutes successful leadership in one place is by no means guaranteed to work elsewhere.

In Scandinavia, for example, the 'law of Jante' is widespread. The concept derived originally from a 1930s novel by Danish-Norwegian writer Aksel Sandemose, *A Fugitive Crosses His Tracks,* in which the inhabitants of the fictional town of Jante decry displays of individualism which threaten to destabilise the harmony of the whole town. There are eleven rules in the law of Jante, all along the lines of 'You are not to think you are any better than the rest of us' and clearly the novel struck a chord with many Scandinavians. Today, managers must seek consensus for any big decisions and plans must be modified until all parties are comfortable with them. The law of Jante is a social contract that determines much of how life is lived in Scandinavia:

reminding people not to think that they are anything special, as in fact *everyone* is special and should be respected.

In Japan, by contrast, the most senior leader in an organisation can expect unquestioning obedience and to be treated with a high level of respect, to the extent that nobody else will even share an elevator with them, unless they are invited to do so. Imagine how confusing it is for young Japanese people who transfer to an Anglo culture where their CEO chats to them in the lift about the football or their plans for the weekend!

The idea of unquestioning obedience is common in many Asian cultures, as it is one of the key tenets of Confucian thinking. Sons always obey fathers, wives obey husbands and younger people will always look up to older people. Although employees will always be happy to be appreciated, they do not expect to be praised for their performance or for working hard – their loyalty is given willingly, in exchange for the 'patronage' of their boss and the opportunities provided. It is both expected and seen as desirable that more senior people keep some distance between themselves and more junior employees, or between a white collar manager and a blue collar factory worker. For many Westerners, this can be very challenging, as Jack found out:

> In Japan, by contrast, the most senior leader in an organisation can expect unquestioning obedience and to be treated with a high level of respect, to the extent that nobody else will even share an elevator with them, unless they are invited to do so.

When Jack moved from Chicago to Shanghai, to take up a role as Managing Director for a sportswear manufacturer, he was keen to understand his new workplace and to put his Mandarin into practice. Stepping outside for a cigarette one day, he spotted some factory employees at the other end of the building and strolled over to join them. After five or ten minutes he went back to his desk, feeling very pleased with himself and the connections he was establishing with the staff, but his Chinese assistant very politely made it quite clear to him that it was not appropriate for senior managers to share their breaks with the factory workers – 'This is China, not America', he was told.

> **In both the USA and Australia, senior people will be given the benefit of the doubt and be treated politely, but they have to earn their status, it is by no means granted automatically.**

In both the USA and Australia, senior people will be given the benefit of the doubt and be treated politely, but they have to earn their status, it is by no means granted automatically. This is not to suggest that Australians will think ill of people until proved wrong; on the contrary they tend to offer everyone a 'fair go', but they are disinclined to give anyone special treatment, such as sitting them at the head of the table or not addressing them by their first names. They treat everyone in the same relaxed manner, no matter who they are. This can of course backfire, when dealing with people who are *used* to being given the red carpet treatment and who are insulted when they don't get it, but it also creates a much more informal workplace where everyone's input is welcome. Even the CEO will greet the office cleaner by his or her first name, unlike other cultures with a much stronger service mentality.

A few years ago, I was due to give a presentation at 7.30 a.m. I was in Melbourne, but working for an Afrikans client. He worked in a fairly

*small building and advised me that I should call him when I arrived,
as I would need a pass to make the lift work. At 7.15 I walked into the
boardroom, much to his surprise.*

'How did you get in?', he asked.

'I asked Peter to help me,' I said.

'Who's Peter? he asked.

*'You know, your Greek cleaner? Very friendly guy, he offered to top up
my parking meter too'.*

*He didn't know, actually. He had worked there for six years and had
never spoken to the cleaner. And Peter had never offered to top up his
parking meter either.*

In the majority of African countries, leaders are expected to behave
like a 'Big Man' and not like everyone else. These men surround
themselves with people who carry out their orders for them and
often treat these subordinates harshly. As Gurnek Bains describes
in his fascinating book *Cultural DNA*, frequently African leaders;

*… can be both paternalistic and caring about their people, while
expecting high levels of respect and obedience in return. In fact,
everybody is strongly attuned to signs of respect and disrespect when
leaders and subordinates engage. These include implicit rules about
how you challenge – or rather don't challenge; how you signal respect;
and how you are expected to wait for prolonged periods to see your
boss, knowing that the meeting may be entirely cancelled on a whim
without the slightest consideration of your feelings. People in an
organization expect their leaders to show confidence and command
respect. In short, they expect them to act like the Big Man.*

He goes on to write elsewhere in the chapter;

In Africa there is a belief in authority and sometimes even quite deeply held superstitious beliefs about the mystical power that those in authority hold. Many African rulers play on these convictions and allow wild rumors to circulate about their prowess and their supernatural skills. Stories about cannibalism are also used to create fear in people. Rulers are frequently perceived by their subjects to have the power to know exactly what everyone is thinking and even at times to be able to control nature and the spirit world.

In stark contrast, in the majority of Anglo cultures and in some European cultures too, there is little sense of respect being 'owed', there is a dislike of anything that sounds like an order, and employees may take offence at any hint of criticism. A French executive commented to me that where the French will describe something as 'pas mal' (not bad) and that French people would be content with this level of praise, Americans want everything to be 'a great or even an *awesome* job'. A Dutch CEO, likewise, found it very difficult to pitch criticism to his Australian staff, as he found that they would become very defensive. The idea of the 'feedback sandwich' was familiar to him, but he described the strategy he finally decided on as 'kiss, kick, kiss'; praise for a great job, followed by a mild suggestion that something might be improved upon, followed by an 'but overall, fantastic job'.

In much of Latin America and Mediterranean Europe, it is both accepted and desired that leaders will demonstrate a very firm, hierarchical management style but this is unlike the type of leadership seen in, say, Vietnam or Thailand, where – as Jack found – junior staff would be very uncomfortable having a more personal connection to their boss. Latin managers are strong guides, but welcome input from junior staff and also like to maintain a strong personal relationship with them. They are warm, personable and likeable and it is not at all uncommon for senior staff to attend family occasions such as weddings and funerals. Family is viewed as more important than work, and relationships with suppliers in these countries will invariably be improved by sharing some stories and photos of your family and enquiring after theirs. Remember Barbara from Chapter 2 and her disappointment at not being invited to the homes of any of her colleagues?

As mentioned above, in India too managers are expected to lead with a firm hand and in return they take an almost parental interest in their employee and even his or her extended family. Arun was an Indian executive who left Mumbai to take up a leadership position in Brisbane and had a difficult time adjusting to local expectations of management. He was reluctant to have any cross cultural training, but five months after his arrival we finally met up. By that time, unfortunately, several stories had reached me of what a 'slave driver' he was, that he had no respect for weekends and evenings, treated most female employees as inferior and thought if the day had 24 hours in it, then at least 18 of them were available for work. Apparently his email and conversational style was brusque, with no pleasantries, and he had generally succeeded in upsetting most of his staff.

'So Arun, what have been your biggest challenges so far?' I asked him.

He scowled, then answered, 'Australians are so lazy and they are impossible to motivate'.

We went on to discuss his personal motivation techniques, which included phoning his staff at 9 or 10 p.m. to discuss the issues of the day when he had thought about them further. He also emailed them several times over the weekend, with long reports attached, and thought it was lazy of them not to reply until the following Monday. Several times he had cancelled the Friday night drinks in order to resolve a small issue, which his team felt could easily have been left until Monday.

I happened to have seen two young Indian men jogging in a park only a couple of weeks earlier and noticed one of them was wearing a backpack. They stopped near me and I heard one man ask the other runner why he needed a backpack. 'I've got my laptop in it, in case my boss calls,' he said. 'He likes me to be available pretty much 24/7, but that's ok, the pay is pretty good and there are lots of opportunities ahead if I put the hours in now. He's pretty tough, but he looks after me.'

The joggers had given me great insight into what Arun's 'normal' was. There are hundreds of thousands of young professionals in India – by 2030 India will supply one quarter of the world's graduates – and they are hungry for success. There is a payoff for dedication shown to their boss; if they work really hard, he or she will look after them and this can make a huge difference to their future success. This was the nature of the workforce that Arun had left behind and one of his challenges as a manager in Australia, was to learn a different way of motivating his people.

Work to Live, or Live to Work?

One of the issues which many expatriates face is moving to a culture which has a different view of the importance and the role of work in people's lives. Cultures tend to either promote a 'live to work' view or a 'work to live' one and this impacts enormously on what might be viewed as someone's 'work ethic'. The notion of Work-Life Balance, for example, is very much a Western construct, with its implicit expectation that these two parts of your life are *separate* – literally at opposite ends of the balance. In non-Western cultures it is much more common for the two to inter-mingle, for people to socialise with their colleagues out of work hours or to work in ways that allow them to combine the two.

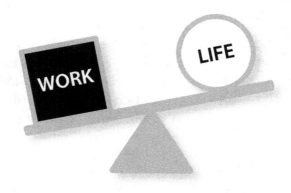

In the 1950s and 60s, when many thousands of Pakistani and Indian immigrants arrived in the UK after Partition, their approach to commerce, for example, was very different to the traditional British way. A typical UK 'corner shop', found throughout the suburbs especially, was generally open from 8am to 5pm only, then 'work' was over for the day. The Indians and Pakistanis and later, groups like the Gujuratis from Uganda, opened their shops earlier and stayed open much later – at least till 10pm. With large family groups, who tended to live together, there was always somebody to mind the shop; Dad could keep an eye on his elderly father while serving out the front, or the daughter could study for her accountancy exams while also selling milk and eggs. As an article by Sudesha Sen in the *India Times* recounts;

> *The East African Gujarati community brought in the corner shop revolution; one that changed forever Britain's antiquated retail laws. The second and third generations have gone on to integrate and succeed, becoming high-fliers and professionals in every walk of British life, from politics to business to finance.*

> Societal expectations about Work-Life Balance are in part influenced by the cultural viewpoint about how much pleasure it is appropriate to have in one's life...

Societal expectations about Work-Life Balance are in part influenced by the cultural viewpoint about how much pleasure it is appropriate to have in one's life – what cross-culturalist Geert Hofstede refers to as the 'Indulgence vs Restraint' dimension. High-indulgence cultures (most of the West, including Australia) place high value on enjoying life, having lots of leisure time and the freedom to follow your own goals and desires. High-restraint cultures tend to think that indulgence must be reined in and that hard work and discipline should be the norm and pleasure just the occasional reward. These values are imposed from early on; in researching cultural expectations of childcare recently, I learnt for example that Chinese parents typically want their child to finish pre-school knowing all their letters and being able to count up to 100, while Anglo-Australian parents see independent play and socialisation as being more important skills to learn.

Japan is often viewed as a culture where people 'live to work'; much of their sense of self is bound up in spending their whole lives working for the same company, knowing their work colleagues very well and feeling very comfortable with the values which their company espouses. In this sense they truly become a 'Mitsubishi Man', in the same way that Scots may say they are a member of the Mackinnon clan or an Australian Aboriginal person might say he is a Wurundjeri man. In India and China, this type of loyalty is also very common and is demonstrated through working long hours, socialising with your work colleagues and being prepared to sacrifice your home life to a large extent.

Traditionally in Asian societies, there has been a societal expectation that women would leave the workforce when they got married in order to care for the home, the family and all the elderly parents. Cracks are, however, starting to appear in this model. Young women who have enjoyed their independence while studying and working overseas are increasingly reluctant to give up their careers in order to stay at home. The costs of caring for all these people are also becoming too much for one bread-winner to cover and for the first time ever in China, aged-care facilities are opening, which enable women to return to paid work.

In countries such as Australia and the UK, Nordic countries and much of Latin America and Africa, a 'work to live' attitude is more common. While people do generally want to enjoy their work and to work for organisations whose values they share, they primarily work in order to get the money they need to enjoy the lifestyle they aspire to. Of course they are still hard workers and will happily stay late in a crisis, but regularly working very long hours and not taking holidays is seen as an imposition on their personal life. In any case, it is felt that people need time to recharge their batteries; during their time out of the office, people can spend time with their families and also contribute to community activities, all of which creates a more balanced society. The Nordic view of the working week is to work smarter, not longer. Denmark is rated as the country with the best work – life balance and the average working day there is 8 a.m. – 4 p.m. and 8 a.m. – 2.30 p.m. on Fridays. The USA is an interesting exception here; although it is changing now, for many years American companies only gave their employees two weeks of annual leave, compared to at least four in other Western societies (and often five or six), they regularly work very long hours and are contactable during vacations.

Applying the Four R's

In this chapter we have considered different styles of management and motivation and started to identify the very real need for 'cultural code switching' if people are to succeed in working across cultures. Being culturally agile requires you to move away from ingrained beliefs about 'how a leader behaves' and to adopt a flexibility in your management style that allows you to be the yin to someone else's yang, whatever that may be. The changes you may want to make must happen gradually and always taking into account the cultural differences. If someone like Robert or Swee-Nor is just not comfortable speaking out, no amount of asking or even instructing them will ever change this, if you don't also invest the time in establishing their trust. If you are asking someone to jump off a high wall, they have to be sure that you will be there to catch them.

How would you apply the **Four R's** to these issues?

Rewards

Questions: Have you ever struggled to be motivated or to motivate a team member? How did you resolve the situation? What could you have done to build trust, to make you more effective and to feel more rewarded?

Considerations: Think back to what you did then to change the scenario – what would you do differently now? How would you reward that team member and what rewards might they offer you?

Research

Questions: What do you need to know about your employees' expectations of you as a leader? How specifically will that help you to become a more effective manager?

Considerations: Trying to teach someone who has a very different learning style can be frustrating; a bit like trying to make a Samsung and an Apple phone work off the same prompts. Learning more about the other persons' culture, including their learning style and what kind of relationship they expect to have with you, will help both of you to have a more productive and more enjoyable relationship.

Reflect

Questions: As a manager, how would you rate the relationship that you have with the members of your team? Do you expect everyone to respond to the same cues? Does your management style work really well with some employees, but not so well with others?

Considerations: Your preferred management style may work with many of your team, but you may have to engage in some 'cultural code switching' to motivate all of them. Remember, this is in no way a comment on the effectiveness of your personal style, but simply a recognition that people learn in many different ways and that you will be most effective if you are willing to accommodate this.

Reach Out

Questions: What strategies do you think will be most valuable in understanding what motivates your employees? What do you need to do to establish a better connection with your team?

Considerations: 'Being Honest' and indeed expecting honesty may not work here; if your unassuming subordinate wants something that you are not giving them, it is unlikely that they will have the confidence to say so. Be willing to switch off your cultural cruise control and make that clear to them; have a frank discussion about how your style may be different and ask what they found rewarding or difficult about their previous manager. If an employee seems engaged and happy but is just not really delivering results, assume cultural differences before anything else and approach this with sensitivity, being mindful of that person's potential to feel shamed by your comments. Remember finally not to take these setbacks personally; you can't really blame your employees as they also need time to adjust to *you*.

Are there any other things to consider in light of what you've learnt from this chapter?

_____

_____

_____

_____

_____

References

- https://www.communicaid.com/cross-cultural-training/blog/indulgence-vs-restraint-6th-dimension

- Gurnek Bains, *Cultural DNA*, Wiley, New Jersey, 2015 pp. 72-75

- http://blogs.economictimes.indiatimes.com/LettersfromLondon/how-gujaratis-changed-corner-shop-biz-in-uk/

- Andy Molinsky ref code switching in *Harvard Business Review*; https://hbr.org/2012/01/three-skills-every-21st-century-manager-needs

- Aksel Sandemose, *A Fugitive Crosses his Tracks,* Alfred A Knopf, 1936

- http://www.theparisreview.org/blog/2015/02/11/the-law-of-jante/

7

All in Good Time
Time & Planning Issues

Different attitudes to time and planning encompass everything from punctuality to multi- tasking and from assiduously planning every detail to embracing a more serendipitous or fatalistic approach to things. They also affect how you see and quantify time and whether you are short or long term in your thinking.

In the Western world, we prefer not to leave things too much to chance and we generally believe that our fate is in our own hands. American advisory service Veritas offers a project management service under the banner 'Sinergy: A methodological approach leaving nothing to fate' and as early as 1587, in Christopher Marlowe's play *Tamburlaine the Great*, Tamburlaine proclaims:

> 'I hold the Fates bound fast in iron chains,
> And with my hand turn Fortune's wheel about'.

In many non-Western cultures, however, this type of boastfulness would almost certainly be seen as *tempting* fate! For people from these countries, there is a widespread belief that the future is largely pre-ordained, so therefore what is the point in trying to force things to happen? In India the sense of karma drives everything and indeed is the fundamental basis of reincarnation. Similarly, the phrase *inshallah,* meaning 'if it is the will of Allah' will be familiar to anyone who has travelled in the Middle East or done business with people from there.

Laura Montini, writing at *Inc.com* notes that

> *Recent research from Duke University suggests that when decision makers are ambivalent about a set of tough choices, they tend to be comfortable pinning the outcome on fate. The researchers defined fate as "the belief that whatever happens was supposed to happen, and that outcomes are ultimately predetermined." They conducted their study by asking 189 participants about their presidential candidate choices during the 2012 election. Those respondents who said they were stumped over their decision were also more likely to indicate that they believed in fate.*

> *If you're thinking that such a philosophy is a little reckless, especially in a business setting, consider the upside. Difficult decisions are stressful and aversive, especially when they're important and need to be made quickly. However, "deferring responsibly for complex issues and attributing events to external forces, such as governments or other powerful forces, can be psychologically palliative and can reduce stress," the authors wrote, citing other researchers in their paper.*

Lawrence T Knight of Beloit College in Wisconsin works in the area of cross-cultural psychology and observes that in fact most Muslim Arabs have a different concept of 'fatalism' than, say, Americans. Fatalism is not an absence of responsibility, but an acceptance of working in partnership with your god. In his blog he quotes a well-known fable told to him by a young Moroccan man;

A man came to visit the Prophet Mohammed and did not tie up his camel. When the Prophet asked the man why he did not tie his camel, the man said, 'There is no need. The Koran says to depend on God.' The Prophet frowned and said, 'First tie it up, then depend on God.'

A colleague who has recently been working in Abu-Dhabi however, told me that while this thinking is somewhat ingrained in the locals' thinking, there is no tolerance for it from Western management. Fate and destiny are inconsistent with Christianity, hence the concepts of *inshallah* and 'karma' (also explored in Chapter 8) are not widespread in the Christian world. Interestingly though the French do have a similar expression, 'La vie s'arrange' which literally means 'Life will take care of itself'. Sounds pretty fatalistic to me, albeit with no religious overtones.

'Slowly, Slowly Catchee Monkey'

The saying 'slowly slowly catchee monkey' dates back to British Colonial times and was the advice given by Indian locals, in pidgin English, to British soldiers trying to catch monkeys to keep as pets. In today's India, the 'slowly, slowly' approach – in other words, resolve issues with patience and care rather than to a deadline – is still often preferred. The belief underpinning this thinking is that deals made in haste could be regretted.

Brad was an American businessman who tried to hasten his Indian clients to 'seal the deal' and found that things didn't go quite as planned. He had thought that being introduced by a mutual colleague would allow him to cut straight to the chase, but despite this, it had taken him months to get to the final stage of making the sale. He had made two trips to New Delhi prior to this one, made numerous calls to his Indian client 'just to be friendly' and eaten more curry than he cared to remember. Now he wanted to clinch the deal…

Brad finished his presentation and turned to his Indian clients with a big smile. He knew he had what they were looking for, now he just had to close the sale. He had heard that Indians could be quite tough negotiators and he must not lose the deal now, it had taken so long to get to this point.

It wasn't like this with his American clients, who like him engaged in a little small talk and then just wanted to get down to business, to figure out the best deal that was mutually acceptable, sign the contract and then move on. They wouldn't necessarily be around in the next quarter, but so long as he reached his targets this quarter, that was the main thing. The Indian client seemed interested in a long-term relationship and Brad wasn't sure he could commit to that; he wasn't even sure he would be with the company next year, but he was determined to get his commission this year.

Brad smiled again at the group of Indian businessmen gathered round the table. 'Now,' he said, 'have I got a deal for you ... you know this piece of machinery is worth $700,000 but I'm prepared to let you have it, today only, for $650,000. This is a fantastic bargain and an offer like this will NEVER be repeated, I am certain of that, so get in quickly! All you have to do to take advantage of this amazing offer is to sign the contract before the end of the day and pay in full in the next 7 days ... So what do you say?'

What the Indian clients said, more or less, was that they would decide when *they* were ready. They wouldn't be rushed into making a decision to suit Brad, on the spurious notion that special offers would 'never be repeated'. Whereas in the West time is seen as something like a conveyor belt, on which every hour moves along and then at midnight slips off the end and the day is never seen again, in places such as India, Pakistan, Bangladesh, Nepal and most of the Middle East too, time is seen as much more like a fanbelt, which loops together the past, the present and the future in an endless loop. Therefore, everything comes round again at some point, it's just a question of waiting until the time is right.

Why the Rush?

Time has a very elastic quality in countries like India, but in Anglo cultures, time is seen as being more quantifiable and having a much more finite quality. Time and money are often linked in the West; expressions such as Benjamin Franklin's now

> In Anglo cultures, time is seen as being more quantifiable and having a much more finite quality.

famous phrase 'time is money' or the concept of 'spending time' are well known. Gold watches are a common retirement gift, to show thanks for the time invested. In China, it is bad form to give someone a clock as a gift at any stage in the relationship, as it suggests that you think the friendship is limited. In South American cultures, it is damaging to the relationship to look at your watch during a meeting and it is also common there for people to arrive late to appointments, because if they bump into someone that they know while on their way to meeting you, they are societally obliged to have at least a conversation with them and quite probably share a coffee too.

Like Brad, Rebecca also found that strong business relationships in many cultures can't be built in a hurry:

At 6 p.m. she wound up her meeting with her Malaysian partners, who were in Melbourne for a few days. After a long day of negotiations, Rebecca was looking forward to a nice glass of wine in the garden with her husband and a bit of time off. She had been to Malaysia two months earlier and met the people involved in her company's joint venture; she'd been out to dinner with them, exchanged gifts, even been taken shopping by their wives and now she just wanted to get on and nut out the details. The Malaysians looked rather affronted when she suggested they should call it a day and that she would see them at 8.30 tomorrow morning, but she made a point of suggesting some nice restaurants they could try and wished them a good evening. They seemed a bit cool with her, but she put it down to tiredness.

In the morning, they were clearly upset with her. Her cheery greetings and enquiries were met with terse replies and several points they had agreed on yesterday were suddenly up for discussion again. The accommodating, flexible nature of their discussions the day before seemed to have disappeared altogether and Rebecca realised she had a long day in front of her.

What did Brad and Rebecca do wrong? To some people nothing, but to others, everything.

In Brad's case, he had not taken into account the Indian view that everything in life runs in cycles and that there was no such thing as a 'never to be repeated offer'. In Rebecca's case, she simply wasn't prepared to invest the time that relationships in Malaysia need if they are to be successful. Like their neighbours in Indonesia and Thailand, the Malaysians do business with people, not organisations, and demonstrating a mutual liking for building a friendly business relationship was critical. Rebecca's attitude of having 'done' the relationship building was all wrong for the Malaysians; the relationship may have been established, but it needed nurturing and cultivating if it were to continue, it is never 'done'. They expected that the kindness they had shown to her in Malaysia would be reciprocated, not just out of obligation, but as a demonstration that Rachel was actually enjoying the relationship and therefore actively wanting to spend time with them. Having to tell their wives that not only had they not had dinner together, but they didn't have any gifts from Rebecca either would have being embarrassing for them.

Both Brad and Rebecca made the mistake of using the style of selling and negotiation that had worked well for them before and expecting it to work the same way in a different context. While they knew that their clients and partners were from a different country, they hadn't done much research and failed to anticipate that their clients might have a different way of doing business. They both mistakenly assumed that because the others dressed in Western style and spoke English, that their behaviours and attitudes would be Western too – so why on earth wouldn't their usual style work for them again?

In for the Long Haul

Japanese company Sony has a 100-year business plan. Many Chinese manufacturers and designers are planning projects that will not come to fruition for another fifty years. Germans too take a long term view, ensuring that manufacturing expansion plans are accompanied by investment in social and educational obligations. All three countries invest heavily in building strong relationships and functional systems, so that goals can be planned for a long way into the future. As with product development (see over) they see no point in going through all the foundation building twice, or in doing something that will only deliver benefit in the short term. Americans, however, and increasingly Australians too, are focused on the next quarterly result or at most on the next five to ten years and often fail to appreciate that not everyone works in the same way.

> Many Chinese manufacturers and designers are planning projects that will not come to fruition for another fifty years.

It is well documented that a very high percentage of American businesses currently investing in China don't see the success they hoped for, during the time frame they have allowed for a return on their investment. As Benjamin Carlson writes in an article on CNBC's website, *Why big American businesses fail in China;*

> Since China opened up to foreign investment in the late 1970s, some of America's most powerful corporations have gone confidently into the People's Republic, only to stagger out a few years later, battered, confused, and defeated.

> "It's a lack of understanding of the legal and cultural environment that leads to most failures," says Shawn Mahoney, managing director of the EP China consulting group. "The only difference between a success and failure in my experience is that people who are successful are more willing to talk and learn about how things work on the ground."

A comparable long-term view is taken of the planning and research undertaken in product development and being a strongly collectivist culture, the Chinese tend to see information as being for sharing, not for keeping to yourself. So while clearly the manufacturing of fake branded goods and the 'borrowing' of other people's intellectual property is a source of huge frustration to the originator, to many Chinese it is the ultimate in practicality – why reinvent the wheel?

As Gurnek Bains writes in *Cultural DNA,* when discussing the relatively common issue of plagiarism amongst Chinese students attending American universities:

> It is important to recognize that plagiarism is much more of an emotive issue in individualistic cultures where the attribution of everything to a person matters. In a more collectivist culture, intellectual property is a collective good. For thousands of years, Chinese scholars have been required to faithfully learn and recapitulate the work of the masters. When Chinese students produce an essay, they are trying to show

they have mastered knowledge in an area. The arrogance of a spotty undergraduate trying to put their own stamp on years and years of work by notable experts is anathema to people brought up in such a tradition, perhaps rightly so.

Although over the centuries many Chinese people have enjoyed having daughters, when the one-child policy was introduced in the late 1970s, many future parents took a longer term view and foresaw problems. Traditionally, sons always stay in the family and the wives they take join the family, which provides among other things care for elderly parents in the long term. Daughters, on the other hand, tend to leave their own parents in order to look to look after their husband's parents. If you were only allowed one child, a daughter might bring you much joy and much help in the shorter term, but in the longer term you would be left with nobody to look after you – hence the preference for boys. (The practice of sex determination and infanticide were both illegal, but by 2020, there will be 30-35 million more men of marriageable age than women).

In much of Africa, however, a short term view is common. The present is seen as very changeable, so what is the point of planning too much or getting angry about your situation? In Kenya, anger is perceived as mental illness and an inability to enjoy what is good in life, so the preferred strategy is to keep looking backwards to your ancestors for guidance but celebrate today with singing and dancing, for who knows what will happen tomorrow. Gurnek Bains refers to research by Walter Mischel on the concept of delayed gratification and notes that due to this unpredictability, Africans are much more likely than Asians to opt for the bird in the hand now rather than a potential two in the bush later. He also refers to African philosopher John Mbiti's belief that (in Bains' words);

... the orientation towards time in Africa is fundamentally rooted in the presence and absence of events rather than having an independent existence; that is, time passes only when events occur. So, if nothing happens, then no time has passed. In Mbiti's view this leads to an orientation toward time in which there is "a long past, a present, and virtually no future." In this context, future events are only anticipated in as much as they fal within the rhythm of natural phenomenon, such as daily fluctuations or the ebb and flow of the seasons.

When viewed from this perspective, waiting hours for a bus or a meeting is not the 'waste of time' that Westerners might see, as theoretically, no time has passed so no time has been lost.

> Throughout history, people from many cultures with harsh climates have taken a shorter term view of things, as their future is so reliant on the weather and therefore is unpredictable.

Throughout history, people from many cultures with harsh climates have taken a shorter term view of things, as their future is so reliant on the weather and therefore is unpredictable. Many people in Russia, Mongolia and much of Eastern Europe for example, were used to packing up and moving on as the weather changed, either up to the pastures to make the most of the spring grass or down to the valleys to avoid the wildest of the winter storms. Life is fragile and your luck can change quickly, so there is no point in too much planning.

Where's Plan B?

In my experience, both the French and German parent companies of Australian subsidiaries are sometimes frustrated by what they see as a lack of detailed planning. In German business, Plan A is always hand in hand with Plan B, it would be foolish to have it any other way. What Australians consider flexibility and the ability to think on their feet, the Germans view as a lack of preparation. There are of course arguments for both approaches. The German attitude would be that it would be far too risky to embark on a project without a back-up plan, a 'Plan B', which can be quickly implemented if necessary. Indeed, more time and planning is required at the start of a project, but things always do go wrong and it is better to be prepared for these eventualities. The Australian view, on the other hand, is much more 'big picture', an overall view of what the project looks like but without all the details finalised. Like the Germans, they acknowledge that things always change and therefore it is good to be able to change your plans as you progress.

In France, a lack of planning is not seen as a learning opportunity, as it is in Australia, but as evidence that the CEO was not up to the job.

Remember Jean-Pierre, the French micro-manager from Chapter 6? One of the other mistakes he made was to insist on his Australian management preparing detailed plans. Not only did he think that this was the 'correct' way to do things, but it also enabled him to know exactly what would happen when, how much it was likely to cost and how long it was likely to take. He was expected to be able to thoroughly brief the executive team in France and without a doubt, forcing his Australian team to plan gave him a level of confidence and security that he would otherwise not have had.

> Forcing your own culture onto a prevailing or dominant culture may work temporarily, but will never work in the long term.

As has been seen many times, however, forcing your own culture onto a prevailing or dominant culture may work temporarily, but will never work in the long term. Jean-Pierre would have had far better results if he had sought to understand why the Australians preferred their style and then incorporated some flexibility into his own style. One of the many benefits of cultural diversity is the diversity of thought that is enabled; doing the same thing in the same way in a new environment is to complete ignore the opportunities that are provided for growth through innovation.

How People Relate to Time

Neuro-linguistic Programming (NLP) is a behavioural science and a coaching methodology which originated in the USA in the 1970s and which I employ in my work. One of its many benefits is to create greater self-awareness, to teach people how to notice the ways in which they receive and process information. NLP practitioners will notice, for example, whether the way in which people describe things is in a predominantly auditory, visual or kinaesthetic way; are they 'on the same page', 'dancing to a different drum' or do things 'just not feel right'?

One of the distinctions made in NLP is whether people are 'In-time' or 'Through-time', which considers how people *see themselves* in relation to time, as opposed to how they apportion their time. People who are In-time are very present, very focused on what they are doing right now, but find it hard to plan ahead, to imagine the consequences of their actions or to think about their issue from multiple points of view. They typically always try and squeeze an extra few minutes out of every hour and rather than get somewhere early, which they would see as a waste of time, they will do something like making a quick phone call which inevitably leads to them running late.

If you have ever walked into someone's office while they are on the phone, and they have completely ignored you – not even acknowledged you – they are almost certainly an In-time person, so engrossed in what they are doing they barely notice you. In-time people typically tend to miss deadlines too and to under-estimate how long projects or travel time will take.

> As an In-time person myself, I'm afraid I am not a very good time-keeper and am always trying to get more out of my day. I called a friend once to say I was running late and would be there 'in a minute'.
>
> 'Is that a real minute or a Patti minute?' she asked. Oops ...

In-time people generally see time as running through their bodies, with the past behind them and the future in front of them. Sometimes the future will be inches from their nose, at other times they can barely see it. But Through-time people will rarely have their timeline 'inside them', instead time will be out the front or either side of them, where they can view it objectively and see how events fit in with other events.

If you imagine time as a brick wall, In-time people see events as separate bricks, while Through-time people view the wall as a whole. How this translates in practical terms is that In-time people will have appointments from, say, 9.30-10.30 and 10.30-11.30 but don't tend to allow a 'gap' for travel time, so they are always late. Similarly, if you think of time as a river, In-time people are standing *in* the river as it flows around them, while Through-time people are standing on a rise looking *over at* the river and watching time flow past. People who are Through-time tend to look at time from afar, they see the past echoed in the present and they see the ramifications of the present in the future. Asked to describe where the future is, Through-time people will generally point to 'over there'. They tend to be very punctual, very organised and frustrated by their In-time colleagues or partners who are always running late.

> Attitudes to time are often personal rather than cultural, but there are nevertheless cultural preferences for behaving one way or the other which predict the national behaviour.

You probably know people from many different cultural backgrounds who are either In-time or Through-time – or sometimes both, depending on the context. Attitudes to time are often personal rather than cultural, but there are nevertheless cultural preferences for behaving one way or the other which predict the national behaviour. People from the USA, for example, with their emphasis on 'opportunity cost' and preference for short-term results, are more likely to be In-time. People from sub-Saharan Africa, on the other hand, tend to be more Through-time, taking a much 'wider' view of things and seeing today's swings and roundabouts as only little blips on the time scape.

As David Livermore writes in *Expand Your Borders*:

> ... there isn't the same concern for efficiency and achievement [in Africa] ... as there is elsewhere in the world. Africans often say to Westerners "You have the watches. We have the time".

Although attitudes are changing as many African nations aspire to become 'first-world' trading partners, there is no doubt that in spite of inevitably *having* clocks, the African view of time is that things happen when they are ready to and the readiness is largely dictated by what happened beforehand. Traditionally, Africans see the future as largely unknowable and therefore focus on the past and the actual, rather than an uncertain future. Trying to plan too far ahead will only result in frustration.

Maria recounted to me her experience of travelling in Tanzania and the 'flexible' nature of the local bus timetables, which happily accommodated unforeseen events,

> In the first few weeks I was there, I always got to the bus stop early, as I would do in Switzerland. In Switzerland, the bus will never wait for you! On one occasion, I ran into a little convenience store to buy a cold drink, explaining that I was in a hurry as the bus was due any minute. Despite my explanation, the girl serving me smiled sweetly at me, carried on singing along to the radio and then sauntered out the back to the fridge. I impatiently drummed my fingers on the counter, keeping one eye on the road for the bus but of course the bus was late anyway, so I didn't need to get so stressed!

Maria concluded that what spending time in Africa had taught her, more than anything else, was to be flexible and to always have a positive attitude. She recognised that there were far too many people in Africa who were *happy* with the uncertain nature of things and that if she were to enjoy her time there, she had to become more comfortable with last minute changes of plan. What she learnt also was the validity of the saying that 'when one door shuts, another opens' and in looking back, reflects that the experiences she enjoyed the most were often those that happened spontaneously.

In a different type of categorisation about people's relationship to time, in 1959 anthropologist Edward T Hall first came up with the terms *polychromic* or *monochromic* cultures and these terms have been in popular usage since the 1970's amongst cross-culturalists. Author and researcher Richard D Lewis describes these types as follows;

> *Germans typified the monochromic group – people who did one thing at a time, usually well, and in a planned order. Italians were classically polychromic, often attempting many tasks simultaneously, displaying more spontaneity, though less process, than their Teutonic neighbours.*

Lewis also explains that, as with Individualists and Collectivists (Chapter 5), the two types are at different ends of multiple spectrums:

> *Linear-active (monochromic) and multi-active (polychromic) cultures are diametrically opposed in nearly all that matters – punctuality v unpunctuality, calm v emotion, logic v intuition, facts v feelings, scientific v flexible truth, loquacity v taciturnity, restrained v unrestrained body language. Almost all areas of activity clash with or irritate exponents of the other category.*

However, Lewis felt that the picture was incomplete and that there were many people who didn't fit into either category, but into a third. These people were typically Asians, whom he describes as: '...less decisive than monochromic people, but more focused than polychromic – [they] rarely initiate action, but prefer first to hear the other side's position and then react to it at their own tempo.'

In his own work, Lewis describes these three types as Linear-active (monochromic), Multi-active (polychromic) and Reactive and he goes on to note that

> In global business, these differences are frequently sources of profound misunderstanding and there is little doubt that linear-active 'powers' (albeit with 50% of global GDP) often lose customers among the 5 billion multi-actives and reactives who are the major markets of the future.

It's not just in 'global business' either that 'profound misunderstandings' occur. I know plenty of couples who are a combination of In-time and Through-time or monochromic or polychromic. Are you the person whose bag is packed hours before you have to leave, or the one making last-minute phone calls all the way to the airport? As an individual, it is very possible to change your default behaviour if it frustrates you, but sadly it is much harder to change someone else's, as Justin has learnt;

Are you the person whose bag is packed hours before you have to leave, or the one making last-minute phone calls all the way to the airport?

> Justin is English and is married to Ana, a Colombian. When I told them about this dimension they both had an 'Ah ha!" moment, as it explained a lot about why they have an argument every time they go to catch a train. Justin's approach was monochromic; 'There is a train at 8.12, so we should leave the house at 8 to allow time to get there and not be rushing'. Ana's approach was polychromic, happy to multitask and view timings as more flexible. Her attitude was 'There's

no need to hassle me, there's always another train. If we miss that one, I'll just grab a coffee or check my emails while I'm waiting'. To Justin, standing about on the platform is wasting time, but to Ana, it's a far more relaxed approach to life.

As far as I know neither of them has changed, but they are still happily married!

Applying the Four R's

In this chapter we have reviewed some of the different ways that people look at time and the impact it has on their behaviours. While the Swiss will never be late for anything and even describe themselves as 'people who eat clocks', the Colombians have a much more laid-back approach to time-keeping. Like all the differences we are exploring in this book, being prepared for them makes managing them a great deal easier. If you know that your Brazilian client is likely to be running late for your meeting, don't plan another one straight after it and do take some reading with you. If you know that you are always running a few minutes late, but have a Japanese client who always turns up 15 minutes early, put the appointment in your diary half an hour before the real time. These are simple and indeed fairly obvious things to do, but often we don't think to do them, because we don't anticipate that people may do things differently to us.

How would you apply the **Four R's** to time and planning issues?

Rewards

Questions: When you think about Rewards, whose attitude to time are you considering? You personally might be thoroughly motivated by a pay rise, but someone else may value the certainty of a 12-month contract much more highly. Are you only offering rewards that would reward *you*, regardless of what approach to time your client or employee may have?

Considerations: Brad was certainly focused far more on *his* rewards than those of his Indian client and it backfired badly for him. Despite the fairly cynical French observation that 'In every relationship there is one who kisses and one who offers their cheek', the relationships that really last will be the ones in which both parties are winners and it may be helpful to reconsider the benefits which you currently offer.

Research

Questions: You have almost certainly noticed that some people you know are always late, always struggle to meet deadlines, are always slow to respond – or maybe that's how *you* are? Have you ever considered that some of your clients and colleagues may view time in a different way to you?

Considerations: As with many of the other differences that have been discussed so far, the way people view time and their relationship to it is never right or wrong, but it can certainly impact hugely on your working relationship with them and make working together enormously frustrating. Learn about the benefits to them of behaving the way they do; maybe they are just doing it out of habit because 'everyone in Rio works like this'. How are these habits viewed in your culture and might it have a reaction that they would not have anticipated? Be prepared to gently point out to them that they 'have spinach in their teeth' and frame the rewards as being for them, rather than for you.

Reflect

Questions: Reflecting is partly about increasing our self-awareness, in order to understand how rewarding it can be to not just tolerate cultural differences but actively embrace them. In this chapter, who has demonstrated this best?

Considerations: Maria from Switzerland is a real success story in the way she consciously chose to shelve her monochromic preferences and slip into a more relaxed way of behaving. Maria had the self-awareness to not only recognise that trying to do anything else was fighting a losing battle, but that it would really make life both easier and more enjoyable to 'go with the flow'. She was, however, only travelling there for a few months and she was on holiday, it is much harder to make these adjustments in a business context, especially if you are a strict time keeper yourself or you have to report to an office full of other strict time-keepers.

Reach Out

Questions: What strategies would be most helpful in addressing time and planning issues?

Considerations: *Your* deadline may be written in indelible ink, but someone else's may be written in pencil and could just be in place as a guide. What is their cultural 'norm' when it comes to deadlines and time-keeping, what is yours, and whose country are you in? While it is important to adhere to your own standards of professional conduct, you can make life very difficult for yourself by insisting on standards that simply are not that important where you now work. Ask what others do, don't assume that you know. Be flexible in your approach and prepared to accommodate a different way of doing things, if that's what works locally. Ensure that if deadlines *are* critical, that colleagues with ESL understand this and understand the consequences for being late. As with resolving so many of these differences, having an honest conversation – about for example, how difficult it is for you having to report to a monochromic head office – will certainly help if people like you and are prepared to make an effort to help you. This won't resolve itself overnight, of course, so 'bend or snap' and don't take it personally – this system works for them even if it doesn't work for you.

Are there any other things to consider in light of what you've learnt from this chapter?

_____

_____

_____

_____

_____

References

- https://www.psychologytoday.com/blog/culture-conscious/201503/are-muslim-arabs-especially-fatalistic

- David Livermore, *Expand Your Borders,* Cultural Intelligence Centre LLC, Michigan 2013, p78

- Gurnek Bains, *Cultural DNA*, Wiley, New Jersey, 2015 p191

- Gurnek Bains reference to Walter Mischel p62 & John Mbiti p64

- Richard D Lewis, http://www.crossculture.com/blog/nationalities/monochromatic-and-polychromatic-cultures/

- Edward T Hall, *The Silent Language*, Anchor Books,1959

- http://www.inc.com/laura-montini/when-you-should-leave-big-decisions-up-to-fate.html

- http://www.cnbc.com/2013/09/26/why-big-american-businesses-fail-in-china.html

8

Lucky for Some
Superstitions & Magic

What role do superstitions, amulets, lucky numbers and magic spells have in modern-day business? You may be inclined to dismiss these things as old wives' tales, but they can in fact be hugely impactful – and not just in emerging markets.

People all over the world have lucky talismans, which range from evil eyes to rabbit's feet and from four-leaf clovers to shark's teeth. Religious relics are particularly popular as talismans; items such as vials of holy water from Lourdes or splinters of wood from the True Cross have always been highly valued amongst Catholics, while in Japan followers of both Shinto and Buddhism buy themselves good luck 'tokens' known as *omamori* to hang in their homes, cars or about their person. Unlike a four-leaf clover, which is believed to bring you universal luck, specific *omamori* are imbued with different 'types' of luck to help you to pass exams, get rich or get married. (Sounds like a great business model!)

> Chinese and Indian people in particular are very keen on numerology and will consult a numerologist to find an auspicious date for weddings, travel, major purchases and yes – the signing of business contracts too.

Many people also have processes and rituals which they go through in particular order, whether they are tennis players who always have to wear particular socks or gamblers who put a lucky mascot on top of their cards.

Dates and numbers can also be lucky – or otherwise. Friday the 13th consistently gets bad press in the West, to the extent that retail sales figures suffer on those days. Chinese and Indian people in particular are very keen on numerology and will consult a numerologist to find an auspicious date for weddings, travel, major purchases and yes – the signing of business contracts too. Numerology is the belief that there is a mystical or other-worldly link between a number and an event. On the website *Lucky Name Numerology,* the author is quite clear about the benefits and risks of doing things at a certain time:

Actions done on [Lucky Days] will confer success. You can begin a business, build a house, change place of work, purchase vehicles, jewellery or properties, travel for work, transact negotiations and settle foe peace [sic].

But equally, if you perform these actions on your unlucky days,

Your actions will result in waste of money, efforts, and time. You may earn a bad name. You may lose your reputation.

Unexpected Delays

Jacques is French and when he moved from France to Manila, to take up the role of CEO for an international company, he was very surprised to learn how much importance his Filipino employees attributed to what he viewed as superstitious nonsense. He was feeling pleased about the bonds he had been building with the local team though. While he had not received any cross cultural training, he had done a bit of research before he went and he understood the importance of maintaining harmony, of not calling out individuals and of building strong social bonds with his team, as well as professional ones. He had noticed that women were poorly represented at the more senior levels, so he was particularly pleased to have been able to offer a promotion to his sales manager, Linda, as it would be a big step up for her. The new job would entail quite a bit of international travel and he thought it would be great for her to get experience of other business cultures. Linda had seemed very pleased when he had offered her the job, but it had now been over two weeks and to his surprise she still hadn't officially accepted it. He decided to ask his Filipino PA Anita if there was something amiss.

'Oh no,' Anita said, 'she is very pleased, but she can't make a decision until the end of the month. It is bad luck to make a decision in October about something that involves travelling overseas and also the moon is at the wrong phase now, she needs to wait until it is waxing to make an important decision about her future.'

Jacques was nonplussed. The Filipino helper they had at their house was reluctant to deal with the ant problem they had, as she believed that black ants in the house predicted a financial windfall, but he hadn't expected such behaviours in a professional environment. However, as Anita said it so matter-of-factly, it made him wonder whether there were other such practices at work?

'Of course, there are lots,' said Anita. 'Do you remember how the girls in the accounts department couldn't stay late to finish that report a few weeks ago? That was because of the ghosts in the trees outside their windows. The trees are actually getting too big, but we can't cut them down or the ghosts will come inside'

When Jacques recounted this story to me, he was clearly still amazed and perhaps feeling a tiny bit superior. Like many people who believe themselves to be entirely free of superstition, he had seriously underrated the extent to which some cultures are influenced by it. What Jacques also failed to acknowledge was that of course the French have their superstitions too – it's just that they call them traditions. I asked Jacques if he would ever have a dinner party with 13 guests, or light three people's cigarettes with the same match? 'Of course not!' he said, 'That would be really bad luck.'

(The origin of both of these French 'traditions' is quite interesting. In Western cultures, the poor reputation of the number 13 is believed to derive from the fact that there were 13 guests at The Last Supper. The match superstition originates from World War I, when keeping a match burning for too long would attract the notice of the enemy sniper.)

Lucky Numbers

Many years ago, before I had even heard of cultural intelligence, I had a Singaporean – Chinese client who had lived in Australia for many years. He always answered the phone 'G'day, Bobby here', and he was a mad fan of Australian Rules Football. He was almost more Australian than many Australians, but I learnt one evening how deeply his cultural roots ran.

I was organising a large fundraising dinner and Bobby had taken a table for his clients. I met he and his guests at the door:

'Welcome!' I said, 'You are on table number four!'

Bobby froze in the doorway with a look of horror on his face and advised that another table had to be found, as he couldn't sit at that one. He was an important guest and I had given him what I thought was the best table, not knowing that the Chinese word for four sounds very like the word for death, and is therefore considered to be very unlucky. Not an auspicious start to a fundraising evening!

There are a number of other superstitions which can impact your working life. Because the number four is unlucky, Chinese people will often prefer to avoid signing important documents on the 4th of the month and the 4th floor is always absent in buildings – often the 14th too. Conversely, the number eight is considered lucky, as it sounds like the word for prosperity. When I tried to book into hospital in Singapore for the birth of our third child, every bed for the 08/08/98 had been booked months previously. In Japan, number eight is also lucky, but both number four and number nine are considered to be unlucky – the word for nine sounds like 'ku', which means to die with pain.

> The Chinese have a number of superstitions which can impact your working life.

In the Western world, the 13th floor is missing in 80 per cent of the world's high-rises; many airports lack a Gate 13 and many airplanes don't have a row number 13. In the UK, houses numbered 13 can be worth up to 1 per cent less than those on either side of them and in Europe generally, Friday the 13th is traditionally seen as a day on which to take extra care – except in Spain, where it is considered lucky.

In India, the Hindu ceremony of *Shradh* occurs during the lunar new year and is a time when people pay their respects to their ancestors. Because people's minds are supposed to be on a higher plane, it is typically a poor time for commercial activity and therefore would be a bad choice of date on which to expect people to sign large sales contracts, open a new business or launch a new product.

> Product marketers should take note that consumers in some countries are more likely to buy products that are packaged in eights rather than fours, for example, and also that some colours are viewed as much luckier than others.

Product marketers should take note that consumers in some countries are more likely to buy products that are packaged in eights rather than fours, for example, and also that some colours are viewed as much luckier than others. A great article in *The Huffington Post* explores what colours mean in different cultures; in Thailand and Japan, for example yellow is considered lucky and to represent both bravery and wealth. In nearby China, however, yellow was the colour reserved for the Emperor and is now associated with pornography. In Western cultures green is associated with spring and new life but in many South American countries, green symbolizes death. Suddenly the colour of your tie or dress can take on a whole new level of meaning.

In many Asian cultures, the first sale of the day is very important as it sets the pace for the rest of the day. When shopping in an Indonesian market, for example, the stall holder will often offer you a special price in order to complete the first sale.

Location, Location, Location

Numbers are also an important aspect of Feng Shui, the Chinese system for ensuring that all aspects of a room or building remain in harmony with each other. At the centre of any Feng Shui consultation is the eight-sided *ba gua* motif or pattern, which emphasises balance and harmony in aspects of design and stipulates design elements such as even numbers of stairs and a yin and yang aspect to every feature. Remember the discussion in Chapter 5 about harmony and the need for balance in everything? 'Qi' or energy is supposedly scattered by the wind, but harnessed by water – hence the preponderance of fish ponds. Water must be standing however, as having a fountain in your house will make your wealth run away.

> Numbers are also an important aspect of Feng Shui, the Chinese system for ensuring that all aspects of a room or building remain in harmony with each other.

In 2012, Chinese company Beiqi Foton Motor acquired a development site in India, in consultation with its Feng Shui practitioner. It was recommended that they find a site with a river in the foreground and a mountain behind it and they found exactly this in a place called Shinde, near the large city of Pune. Although Feng Shui is dismissed as superstition by the Chinese government, Foton executive Mr. Zhao had noted that 'there is a river, should be good Feng Shui' and the company was keen to progress. Unfortunately for the Chinese, the site was already a sacred site for Hindus and they were adamant that the site should not be tampered with in any way and that pilgrims should be able to access the site whenever they desired.

As Keith Bradsher wrote in a fascinating article in *The New York Times*:

> The culture clash was immediate.
>
> Foton erected barbed-wire fences and hired uniformed guards to keep out trespassers. Cattle herders and Hindu pilgrims have repeatedly trampled the fences. The monks do not want a noisy neighbour.
>
> 'In today's life, spirituality and science are both important, and neither should deny the other,' Kailash Nemade, a monk, said during a pause from chanting religious poems. 'But this factory should not come here, because it will ruin the spirituality of the mountain.'

It is not uncommon in China for religious sites and even whole suburbs to be displaced to make way for new factories and roads, but since acquiring the land in India three years ago, very little has happened. The company's progress in developing the site has been very slow and it now looks increasingly unlikely that plans will be fulfilled as intended. India is by no means the only challenge either; the Chinese are finding it much harder to impose their demands on locals in a number of South American and African countries too. As Bradsher also observes:

> Chinese companies have embarked on ambitious overseas expansion efforts, snapping up land in dozens of countries to build factories, industrial parks, power plants and other operations ... [but] ... are struggling to navigate complex cultural, political and competitive dynamics.

Before making assumptions that superstition tends to impact only one half of the globe, it is worth noting that partial eclipses have an impact on the stock market performance. A *Harvard Business Review* article called 'Why Superstition Works in Business' refers to research by Copenhagen Business School's Gabriele Lepori, which matched the incidence of partial eclipses against the performance of four American stock indices. Lepori noted a small but persistent slump around the time of the 'bad luck' associated with the eclipse.

Fatalism & Karma

Although not strictly 'superstition', in many cultures – and particularly those where religion has a strong influence – there is an unshakable belief that our fate is not in our own hands. In these cultures, which include most of the Asian, African and Middle Eastern countries, our destiny – including the outcome of potential business deals – is part of a much bigger plan that our God or the universe has for us. This concept was also discussed in the Chapter 7, *All in Good Time*, but like many of the topics in this book, it can be considered from more than one angle.

Although not strictly 'superstition', in many cultures – and particularly those where religion has a strong influence – there is an unshakable belief that our fate is not in our own hands.

Between all people there is a sense of 'Do unto others as you would be done by', but in Hindu and Buddhist countries such as India and Thailand, this is taken much more literally than in, for example, Germany or America. It's one thing to treat others well because it is the right thing to do, but it is quite another to feel that there will actually be consequences if you don't.

The Buddhist and Hindu concept of Karma is defined by the Oxford Dictionary as 'the sum of a person's actions in this and previous states of existence, viewed as deciding their fate in future existences'. In other words, your present actions will determine your future state. It's up to you whether you want to be a dung beetle or a sacred cow in your next life; if you are holy and generous and selfless in your actions now, you will be rewarded in this life or in your next incarnation.

Karma: 'What goes around comes around'.

Karma is soundly based on the concept of reincarnation, but because the Bible stipulates that '… man is destined to die once, and after that to face judgement', the concept is rejected by Western theologians and widely dismissed in Western cultures as a result. While certainly there are many references in the Bible to reaping what you sow, in contemporary Western cultures the reward is very much expected in this world, not in the next, particularly as the Western world becomes more and more secular. While the prospect of eternity in either Hell or Heaven would have been persuasive in older times, typically rewards in the here and now are of more interest, although this does not of course mean that the focus on rewards is entirely financial.

The Middle Eastern concept of *inshallah* literally means 'If Allah wills it' and, while not a superstition, is similarly other-worldly. A website called *The Blue Abaya* notes that while *inshallah* used to be a statement of positive intent, it is now used far more often as an excuse to avoid doing something:

> Within the workplaces in KSA [Kingdom of Saudi Arabia], where multiple nationalities and cultures mix, inshallah has caught on a negative connotation...The saying is commonly used and abused by expats and Saudis as well ... Inshallah is generally used to brush things off as unimportant or insignificant. When there are no intentions to actually perform a task, a plain inshallah is the most common response. Inshallah is used as a sort of 'buffer' to soften what the person really wants to say; 'NO'.

Inshallah is often used as an opportunity to *not* make a decision about something. If deciding against something might cause embarrassment or disappointment to someone, it is better to let 'someone else' decide and absolve yourself of the responsibility. The phrase inshallah is literally used for everything from discussing the weather, to determining whether a taxi driver can actually take you to your destination, to whether or not a baby will survive an illness. As noted above, it is also widely used in business contexts too. Although theoretically the growth of Western management and leadership styles do not tolerate this approach, it will take many years for such an ingrained tradition to lose currency.

The Magic of Africa

There are multiple words for magic, from different African langauges and countries, including *mojo, obeah, palo, voodoo* and *hoodoo*. The word *Juju* originally came from West Africa, but is now used widely across Africa to describe all kinds of magic, good and bad. People from many African countries feel a very strong connection to the spirit world and *juju*, or magic of some kind, is the explanation for everything which cannot be explained by rationale means, whether it is the star football team losing, the local well drying up or your business suddenly taking a turn for the worse. Recognition of *juju* may involve simply making small donations at a shrine, wearing significant beads or the saying of a particular phrase, but *juju* can also have a much darker side, with a role in ritual medicine for example.

Of course, the head of a manufacturing plant whom you visit in Botswana or the tea plantation owner you consult in Kenya will be highly unlikely to display any *obvious* signs of *juju*, but it may well be a factor in determining the outcome of your visit because, as Gurnek Bains notes:

> A Gallup survey in 2010 found that across Africa some 50 percent or so of people believed in witchcraft ... [and] one sees the impact of these beliefs in the business world as well. When things go wrong, people are reluctant to blame their immediate team – but can be motivated to find malignant influences from other parts of the organization. These beliefs can interfere with the drive to find more rationale explanations.

> It is interesting to note also that up to **95 per cent** of Africans believe in witchcraft, with higher rates of belief in West and Central African countries...

It is interesting to note also that up to **95 per cent** of Africans believe in witchcraft, with higher rates of belief in West and Central African countries, as was also reported in an article on the website *Livescience*. Overall, there is a very strong sense of the prevalence of the spirit world – both the spirts of one's ancestors, as well as the spirits of geographical features and weather – in everyday activities. Many Africans believe that Westerners just don't see the connection and in that sense, as Bains writes, 'are blind to the power of deeper forces and how interconnected the world is'. With the mining industry being such an important factor in Africa's growth and with the high percentage of unskilled labour employed in it, a workforce influenced by *juju* in one form or other could easily have very costly ramifications for the uninformed.

Applying the Four R's

In this chapter we have explored some concepts not normally considered in most Western workplaces. However, as the East and West draw closer together and people increasingly work across both cultural extremes, it becomes ever more important to understand the factors which may influence our Indian, our Nigerian or our Chinese colleagues' decisions. Like so many of the behaviours we have covered in this book, you can probably get away with ignorance for a while, but understanding how other business cultures operate will ultimately be of great personal and professional advantage to you.

How would you apply the **Four R's** to some of the issues raised here and which you may yourself have come across?

Rewards

Questions: In situations characterised by what may seem to be quite illogical factors, do you need to recalibrate what a 'reward' looks like? If financial rewards have got to be a longer-term goal for you, what other kind of rewards are more easily accessible to you in the short term?

Considerations: Conducting business in places like Africa and Asia offers a fascinating learning opportunity for anyone wishing to grow their cultural intelligence and become more effective at communicating across cultures. Console yourself for the sometimes frustratingly large amount of time invested in building strong relationships with the knowledge that these emerging markets are the economic powerhouses of the future and you are getting in ahead of the game.

Research

Questions: How likely is it that you would be able to learn about these sort of issues from books and the internet?

Considerations: While you will easily find reference to auspicious numbers and unlucky colours, some of these issues will be less visible as they fall into the category of 'old wives' tales' and are therefore often dismissed as being unimportant. As well as doing what research you can, you should certainly consider asking the locals too, and checking with other expats who have been there for a while about what things surprised them. Jacques noted to me that he had not come across *any* reference to the widespread nature of superstition in all his reading. He would have done well to take his PA out for lunch on day one and pick her brains about local issues.

Reflect

Questions: What might be some barriers that prevent you from seeing notions of superstition, *juju*, numerology and so on as serious issues?

Considerations: The world is divided into those who believe without question and those who require empirical evidence. If you are in the latter group, you may find it very challenging to take these issues seriously, but bear in mind that if any hint of your scepticism is apparent, the people you interact with may be extremely insulted. Whatever the situation is, try to keep an open mind. Imagine too, how hard it might be for junior staff in particular, if they are asked to dismiss something which they have spent their whole life believing in and which will probably still be reinforced at home.

Reach Out

Questions: What strategies would be most helpful to you in this case?

Considerations: Probably the biggest issues here will be that the information might be hard to unearth and your default response to it might be to not take it seriously. You may have to engage Sherlock on overtime and make it very obvious that you are interested, but not judgemental; whether you feel that it's superstitious nonsense or not is irrelevant. Explore the reasons why these beliefs exist, they can be fascinating. Do some research into your own superstitions or traditions too and share these in conversations with new colleagues. Why, for example, in Western cultures, are horseshoes a symbol of good luck and a black cat a harbinger of bad luck? Why don't we walk under ladders or look at the new moon through glass? Switch off your cultural cruise control and you'll see it's not just 'them', it's all of us!

Are there any other things to consider in light of what you've learnt from this chapter?

_____

_____

_____

_____

_____

References

- www.lucky-name-numerology.com

- http://www.nytimes.com/2015/12/31/business/international/a-chinese-company-in-india-stumbling-over-a-culture.html?_r=0

- http://www.huffingtonpost.com/smartertravel/what-colors-mean-in-other_b_9078674.html

- *Why Superstition Works in Business* https://hbr.org/2011/01/why-superstition-is-good-for-y

- Gurnek Bains, *Cultural DNA*, Wiley, New Jersey, 2015 pp 68

- http://www.blueabaya.com/2010/12/abused-inshallah.html

- http://www.livescience.com/8515-belief-witchcraft-widespread-africa.html

9

Etiquette Matters
Appearances & Hierarchy

These final two chapters are intended to make you think about cultural differences with a very personal outcome in mind – your own ability to establish a genuine connection with your culturally diverse colleagues and clients. In this chapter, therefore, we will discuss what your appearance says about you to others and we will also talk about forms of address and the importance of observing the local hierarchy. In the next chapter, we will discuss how to build strong collegial and client relationships.

It can be safely assumed that when people seek to establish any kind of business based relationship – whether as an employee, a provider or a purchaser – it is primarily to enable the delivery of goods or services, within an agreed time frame and at an agreed price, to mutual advantage. This is, however, only the bare minimum; the really rewarding and long-lasting relationships are those in which there is mutual professional regard *and* when people actually like each other. Liking someone is what makes us happy to go the extra mile for them. Clients who *like* you are more likely to value your service and to pay your bills on time. Colleagues who like you will willingly pull out all the stops to help you make a tight deadline.

> When joining an overseas office – whether for a few days or a few years – working out how to do the job is only one of many considerations.

When joining an overseas office – whether for a few days or a few years – working out how to do the job is only one of many considerations. Equally important in those first few weeks is connecting with your colleagues or clients on a personal level and to be able to do that, you have to fit in. Many of the things which you took for granted before suddenly have the potential to become issues for you;

• Maybe you enjoy complimenting your female colleagues on their appearance, but none of the other men seem to do this.

• Everyone in your new office uses first names, but you feel it is disrespectful if subordinates don't address you by your title.

• Perhaps you like to eat lunch at your desk, but people think you aren't very friendly when you don't join them in the café or the canteen.

• You are used to having someone serve you coffee, but now you not only have to make your own, you have to wash up your own cup too!

• In your previous job, you only ever visited clients with your boss, but now you are expected to attend on your own.

- You were used to having your own support staff, now you have to share one assistant with three other people.

There are all sorts of – unfortunately, largely *unwritten* – rules, which we gradually observe and then take on board, as few people are happy to be the odd one out. Especially if you are there as an expatriate, feeling that this is a team you can belong to and that everyone is prepared to make you welcome puts a little spring in your step and helps you through those first few difficult months. Learning the local 'office etiquette', no matter how long or short your stay is, will without doubt make your time there more enjoyable.

It may be possible, after people have got to know you better, that you'll be able to wear that floral tie after all or that you won't be thought of as unfriendly if, a couple of times a week, you go to the gym at lunchtime instead of to the café, but insisting on doing these things at the start may not win you any friends. Initially, it will pay off to try and adopt the local behavior as much as you can. We only have one chance to make a first impression – and a very short one at that – so why risk blowing it?

> It may be possible, after people have got to know you better, that you'll be able to wear that floral tie after all or that you won't be thought of as unfriendly...

Dressing to Impress

There is no doubt that people judge and evaluate us by the clothes we wear – this is why it takes some of us so long to get dressed in the morning! Sometimes, unfortunately, your preferred dress style does not translate across cultures and what you view as both comfortable and professional, or perhaps a little arty or creative, is met with some disapproving looks. The Australian and British men's fashion for pairing coloured and patterned shirts with a tie of contrasting colour or pattern, for example, is far too vibrant for many Asian business communities, as are the brightly coloured socks also worn. Business men in Asia will typically favour a much more modest look for the office, such as a white shirt and a plain tie, worn with a black suit.

> In collective societies such as China and Japan, dressing the same way as everyone else is another way of not standing out from the crowd...

In collective societies such as China and Japan, dressing the same way as everyone else is another way of not standing out from the crowd, although *young* Japanese people wear some of the most eccentric and bizarre clothes in the world – perhaps getting it out of their system before they join the ranks of 'salary men' in their black suits. ('Salary man' is the term used to describe the thousands of young Japanese men who join large corporations upon leaving university, then slowly and steadily work their way up through the ranks. Their preference is to toe the company line and do everything they can to avoid being singled out for anything other than exceptional performance.)

Sending the Wrong Message

A common issue for Western women going to work in more male-dominated cultures is that they may not have the freedom to dress as they have always done. The film *Erin Brockovich* sent a clear statement to American audiences about a woman's right to dress as she chose in the workplace, but in cultures used to seeing women dressing more modestly, this will not benefit you in the long term. You may be within your rights, but you will still be made to feel uncomfortable.

A few years ago, I trained a young Australian woman called Rachel, who was moving to Kuala Lumpur with her job. When we met, she was wearing a striking hot pink dress. It fitted closely around her waist and hips, with a deep V at the front. Rachel knew she looked sensational, but what she didn't know was that to her new Malaysian clients, she would be seen to be offering a lot more than just IT solutions!

At her cultural debriefing in Sydney, I addressed the way Rachel dressed. I approached it from various angles, advising her that Malaysia is a predominantly Muslim country and that while not fundamentalist, most women there wore at least a hajib and many wore a burqa or a niqab. We also discussed the fact that business was very male dominated, that a lack of modesty was seen as a lack of morality and so on, but she failed to see the connection with how she herself was dressed. She was quite certain that with her product knowledge and experience it would not be a problem. Finally, I had to be quite blunt with her and advise that not only would she struggle to be taken seriously as a business development manager, but she may get frequent requests for additional business services which she had no intention of offering.

On some occasions, of course, you can do everything possible to prepare but still be caught out unawares. Moira had an interesting experience in nearby Indonesia, where young women can, and in fact often do, show a lot of leg, although they rarely show any cleavage. Older women's dress is expected to become a lot more conservative and skirts should definitely be longer. As a very senior Australian businesswoman, Moira certainly dressed as an older woman was expected to, but she was still caught out.

Because there are relatively few senior businesswomen in Indonesia, Moira found herself going to restaurants with clients in the evening where the men's tradition was often to sit on very low stools or cushions and eat off a low table. While the men would typically sit cross-legged, Moira could obviously not do this in a skirt, nor could she point the soles of her feet towards anyone as this would be considered extremely rude. She either had to sit with her legs bent in front of her, or kneel, or kneel to the side – all of which involved either a significant loss of modesty or terrible cramp in her hips!

Moira did appreciate, however, that her Indonesian hosts would be hugely embarrassed if they knew how awkward this was for her, so with several gracious smiles but minimum fuss, she was able to acquire several large cloths with which to preserve her modesty. Thereafter, she always remembered to wear more voluminous skirts ...

Simon was also caught out in Indonesia; as a man he was invited to attend the local mosque but in taking his shoes off at the door, he revealed not just that his toes were showing through the end but also that he was not wearing a matching pair of socks. Always slightly scruffy anyway, he said he felt very embarrassed alongside so much pressed white linen.

> In most of the world's cultures, your clothing sends a message about both how highly you value yourself and the respect you have for those around you.

In most of the world's cultures, your clothing sends a message about both how highly you value yourself and the respect you have for those around you. Responses to people dressing 'differently' are deeply ingrained and may surprise you sometimes. In Australian writer Sarah Turnbull's book *Almost French*, she recounts how horrified her French boyfriend was at her attempt to go to the bakery in her tracksuit one early Sunday morning. While in her view it didn't matter what she looked like, in his view it was insulting to the baker not to make more effort to look nice in his shop, when he had gone to such efforts to bake delicious bread! My English colleague Sylvie remembers turning up to see the company doctor in Milan and being stunned to see her wearing a leather skirt and fishnet stockings. Clearly from the doctor's point of view, being a doctor didn't mean she couldn't enjoy being female too, but Sylvie was ashamed to admit that her default reaction was firstly to assume that the doctor was actually the receptionist and then to question the woman's professionalism.

On a lighthearted note, beware of buying local clothing with messages and slogans in languages that you can't read and which you might end up wearing while you are there, for instance to an informal company get-together. If you are lucky, the message will only read something innocuous but inconsequential, but you can't always be sure. I bought a t-shirt in Mongolia that apparently said something fairly risky and I saw a nun I saw in Tokyo with an interesting handbag, featuring a picture of a pretty young woman and the words 'I Love Lesbians'.

Casual Clothes Day has been widely adopted by Australian and other Western workplaces, but it is not common in Asia or in many European countries and certainly it is something that one must be aware of when working with clients from other cultures, but meeting on your home ground. In Japan, your professional integrity and worth would almost certainly be questioned if you do not 'look the part' to them. Chinese clients will also expect their providers to dress very smartly and will not be impressed by the wearing of 'casual clothes'. In some Australian

> In Japan, your professional integrity and worth would almost certainly be questioned if you do not 'look the part' to them.

offices, 'casual clothes' can simply mean not wearing a tie for men or not wearing heels for women, but in many others – and particularly in the summer – it seems to be code for a much more dress-down approach. This is often a source of great confusion for expatriates. Several European clients have commented that they find the outfits worn on casual clothes day to lack professionalism and be more suited to going to a beach or nightclub.

> My advice to both men and women is always to err on the side of caution; it far better to be overdressed than underdressed...

My advice to both men and women is always to err on the side of caution; it far better to be overdressed than underdressed and much more relaxing to just take the jacket and tie off, rather than spend the whole day wishing you had worn one.

When in Rome ...

Is it ever appropriate to wear the local dress? It really does depend on a number of things and it is perhaps easier for men to adopt the local fashions than for women to, partly because the men's clothing tends to be less flamboyant anyway. In India, for example, most men will be comfortable wearing a Nehru-style collarless shirt. In Hong Kong and Singapore, many of the expat men wear Chinese style tuxedo jackets with a Mandarin collar. Most women though would find wearing a sari – let alone tying one – a real challenge, as it also demands a different way of sitting and walking. Most Western women will also prefer to avoid wearing a top and skirt combination that can leave a spare tyre or two on show round the waist, but in the same way that French women seem to be able to transform a casual outfit with the addition of an artfully tied silk scarf, Indian women add grace and beauty to their outfits with a drape of silk gauze and an armful of gold bangles, which can be hard to pull off without a lifetime of practice.

However, it is sometimes expected in India that expatriate women will wear a sari and as Narelle Hooper wrote in the *Australian Financial Review*, one American expatriate came up with a novel solution to this problem. Northparkes Mines boss Stefanie Loader explained to Hooper what happened;

> *'I went to India in 2008 to the Bunder diamond project in Madhya Pradesh. We did a number of things to broaden and localise our workforce. We had a women's-only workshop and talked about social programs and employment. I said, "How about driving?" We started with a group of 14. I said, "Righto, I've been driving a car since I was 16. You guys have been wearing saris since you were six. Test me and I'll test you."*

> *I got a couple of the ladies to give me pointers and they did their driver training program.'*

Definitely a win-win.

Accessories & General Appearance

Accessories and general appearances are also very important to consider. Many European men have manicures as a matter of course and they see nothing feminine in this. Indeed, they would look askance at a man or a woman with untidy nails and – heaven forbid – unpolished shoes. They also find it immensely practical to carry their wallets, phones and keys in what Anglo men refer to rather derisively as a 'man bag', but

> Many European men have manicures as a matter of course and they see nothing feminine in this.

which any Italian man would tell you if infinitely preferable to spoiling the line of their expensive suit.

In Europe, clothes and accessories should be stylish but somewhat understated and not designed to bring attention to the wearer. In Switzerland, Germany and many other European countries, the type of ostentation and deliberate display of wealth popular in some of the Asian cultures is considered crass; the emphasis is on high quality rather than fashionable brands. But, it's all personal, and in many cultures having the right accessories is hugely important and the accessories are definitely there to be noticed. Junior staff in Hong Kong will save for months to have a Gucci bag or a pair of Chanel sunglasses, as the wearing of expensive brands is a real status symbol and – more than just a fashion trend – is a demonstration of their success. These brands must of course be the real thing – fake versions do not pass muster!

> Possessions are one of the easiest ways to show off your wealth, but you have to know when to do it and when not to do it.

Possessions are one of the easiest ways to show off your wealth, but you have to know when to do it and when not to do it. In Australia, someone flaunting their expensive belongings would be viewed by many people as 'having a ticket on themselves' and trying too hard to impress, but in places like Shanghai and Beijing, the mega rich eschew humble BMWs and Mercedes in favour of Lamborghinis and Ferraris. There are several very exclusive 'Millionaires' Clubs', each more fabulous than the last. In Mongolia, I was amazed to see a Hummer Club and the most successful Louis Vuitton store worldwide is in Ulan Bator. In Singapore, many wealthy locals build large homes on the corner of busy intersections, so that people can see how successful they have been and how many prestige cars they have parked in the driveway.

Clothing, accessories and appearance generally may not be that important to you, but if they are important to your new colleagues or client, you may well be judged by them early on in your relationship. And it is worth remembering that this judgement may take place in as little as seven seconds – hardly enough time to extend your manicured hand! – as Carole Kinsey Gorman describes in *Forbes Magazine*:

> Clothing, accessories and appearance generally may not be that important to you, but if they are important to your new colleagues or client you may well be judged by them early on in your relationship.

> *You meet a business acquaintance for the first time – it could be your new boss, a recent addition to your team, or a potential client you want to sign up.*

> *The moment that stranger sees you, his or her brain makes a thousand computations: Are you someone to approach or to avoid? Are you friend or foe? Do you have status and authority? Are you trustworthy, competent, likeable, confident?*

> *And these computations are made at lightning speed — making major decisions about one another in the first seven seconds of meeting.*

Unfortunately, you cannot stop the other person from going through this rapid decision-making process, but you can do your research so that you know what factors will work in your favour and what won't. Remember that a lot of articles such as this *Forbes* one are written from a very Western perspective and encourage you to make lots of eye contact and to be enthusiastic and self-confident. These things don't succeed everywhere, so look at articles that relate to the country you are visiting in order to give yourself the best chance.

Hierarchy & Formality

What's in a Name?

Australians don't stand on ceremony and are well known for referring to almost everyone by their first name – if they don't call them 'mate'. This is a reflection of the Australian love of egalitarianism, but it is not necessarily something that is shared or welcomed by all. It can be hugely insulting for people from both more hierarchical cultures and more formal societies to suddenly find themselves being addressed as equals.

> Most Europeans would never presume to calling a professional person with academic qualifications by their first name; even after working together for ten or fifteen years...

Most Europeans would never presume to call a professional person with academic qualifications by their first name; even after working together for ten or fifteen years, people in Switzerland will still address each other as Herr or Frau. People must wait to be invited to use the familiar form of address and this can be rescinded on occasion too, if circumstances change. Often *all* qualifications are voiced and people can end up being addressed as 'Herr Doktor Professor Braun'. It isn't always the case and things are changing slowly, but imagine how taken aback the Herr Doktor Professor Braun might be, when the receptionist at the Sydney subsidiary greets him with a 'Hi Wolfgang, how was your weekend?'

Being too formal can also be an issue. In the southern states of the USA, it is still common for Sir and Ma'am to be used and for people not used to it, this not only seems incredibly old fashioned but also has the unintended consequence of making people feel ancient. If people *are* older, it may well be quite appropriate; older people in most cultures feel more respected when addressed more formally, and in business dealings, failure to accord someone this respect will be frowned upon. In the Philippines, too, 'Sir' and 'Ma'am' are still widely used. Remember Jacques from the Chapter 8? Originally from France, he had spent five years in Australia before going to Manila and found he had to recalibrate his 'normal' again:

> *'When I first arrived in Australia,' he told me, 'I couldn't believe that everyone addressed me as Jacques – in France only my very senior colleagues would use my first name. After a while though, I got to like it; I thought it was friendly and good for breaking down barriers. Now I've gone to the Philippines and they all want to call me 'Sir', which I really don't like but which they like. So, we've come up with a compromise – Sir Jacques! And I'm quite liking the sound of that!'*

Degrees of seniority and societal hierarchy are reflected in many languages, but not English, making it hard to remember sometimes that if you are speaking one of these language (French or German, for example), close colleagues may be addressed using the informal pronoun ('tu' or 'du'), but older and more senior people but others must always be addressed using the formal one ('vous' or 'Sie'). This is starting to change in France now, but not in Germany or Switzerland, where the more informal form of address would only ever be used between good friends – so you won't go wrong if you address everyone as 'Sie'. Interestingly, the formality of the address can also change depending on which language is being spoken; a Swiss client, for example, calls his CEO Herr Muller when they speak German, but Karl when they are speaking in English. In South Korea, unfortunately, you have *multiple* chances of getting it wrong, as there are six different forms of address, dependent on the level of your relationship.

As with so many of the etiquette issues discussed in this chapter, observe what people of the same seniority are doing and follow suit. When people are ready, they will invite you to use their first names. As with your clothing, it is always better to err on the side of being too polite, rather than not polite enough and far better to be viewed as old-fashioned than ignorant.

Going up?

Many years ago, I was working in London and my managing director found me crying in the lift one day. I was only a few years out of university and had let a storm in an office teacup turn into a tempest. Far from adding to my embarrassment, 'Mr. B' rode up and down in the lift with me for the next ten minutes, listening to my story and helping me to resolve the situation. I have thought of his kindness often over the years, but 24-year-old Yori, from Japan, was not so lucky. We met initially in Australia, when she was studying at business school in Melbourne but since then she had moved back to Japan and started working for a large company there. She emailed me after a couple of months and wasn't happy with the differences she was experiencing:

> *'As just an intern in Melbourne, I was on first name terms with all the senior managers and clients and even socialised with them sometimes, but it's not like that in Japan. There is hardly any joking around and everyone is so worried about what everyone else will think of them! I hardly ever even see the MD and if I do, I can't have a normal conversation with him the way we did in Melbourne. I'm not even supposed to share the lift with him, unless he invites me to join him – it's crazy.'*

Privileges such as not having to share the lift with anyone also extend to palatial offices, expensive cars and having staff to make coffee and do your typing for you. Younger Westerners might find it hard to imagine a workplace where this happens, as these types of benefits are rarely given in Anglo cultures any more, other than in some family companies and for very senior people. Instead, offices become more and more open plan, few people have a door on their office and workplaces have self-serve kitchens with signs reading things like

> 'Put your cup in the dishwasher
> – your Mother doesn't work here'.

It can be difficult to strike the right balance, as an Italian client who had spent time working in New Delhi told me;

'People were very upset with me when I brought my own little coffee machine into my office' he said. 'Senior managers do not make their own drinks there, there are tea boys to do that, just like there is someone to clear the cup away. But it was a problem for me, as the coffee was undrinkable!'

His simple but effective solution was to show the tea-boy how to use the machine.

Max, from Holland, spent a few years working for a multi-national in Portugal and found that communication between the various departments was not good. Despite the companies' offices in other countries having dispensed with obvious executive privilege, in Portugal it was still very prevalent, as Max explained;

There were still a great many private offices, each one with a fierce executive assistant who controlled the diary and access to the executive concerned. Decisions were made over long lunches, people's personal networks were far too influential and too many heavy doors remained shut to anyone trying to do things differently. I was naturally not very popular when I arranged to literally tear down the walls, introduce weekly team breakfasts and restricted the use of company credit cards, but the Portuguese operations have improved considerably as a result of these changes.

Many global companies are currently in transition from one style to another, which is cause of further confusion. In addition, company culture is not set in stone (whatever the HR team might think); many of the expatriates I have worked with have arrived feeling confident that they would fit right in, because they worked for the same company at home, but of course the 'personality' of different country offices is based not just on the corporate culture but also on what is deemed acceptable behaviour in the context of the national culture. Being a manager in the USA, for example, may involve many different responsibilities to being a manager in Taiwan.

Achievement vs Ascription

One of the reasons that executive privileges are considered either *so* important or, to some, so completely *unimportant* is to do with another cultural dimension which cross-culturalists Charles Hampden-Turner and Fons Trompenaars refer to: Achievement vs Ascription. This explores the notion of how status is awarded. In Achievement cultures, like Nordic and Anglo ones, you are awarded status based on what you personally have achieved or accomplished. In Ascription cultures, status is awarded based on what you

> One of the reasons that executive privileges are considered either *so* important or so completely *unimportant* is to do with another cultural dimension...

have had the good fortune to be born with or given; for example your gender, your inherited wealth, your family name, having attended the 'right' school and so on. In other words, people are judged either on what they have made of themselves or on what others have made of them.

The British upper class was always very much of the Ascription mindset, with the school that you attended being more important than the academic results which you got there. This *is* changing quite rapidly, but it is still not uncommon for one of the first questions asked of you at a cocktail party to be about which school you attended. One hundred or even fifty years ago, a pop-star and a football player would never have been invited to a royal wedding, but David and Victoria Beckham took their places quite comfortably amongst the aristocracy at the wedding of William and Kate. Arguably, they are the 'new royalty' themselves and in this sense, their achievements have been allowed to outweigh their non-aristocratic beginnings.

American society, on the other hand, has always been an Achievement culture, in the way it celebrates the self-made man and sees 'new money' as being just as good as 'old money'. Indeed, the basis of the American Dream is that people can arrive with nothing and with enough determination and hard work, can transform their lives. One of the reasons for the incredible popularity of the Kennedy family is arguably that they personify this dream; family members arrived with nothing after fleeing the Irish potato famine, but gradually established successful

> American society, on the other hand, has always been an Achievement culture, in the way it celebrates the self-made man and sees 'new money' as being just as good as 'old money'.

businesses, acquired great wealth and ultimately a Kennedy became a president of the United States.

Within business cultures, an Ascription-oriented people such as the Chinese use titles to clarify the person's place in the hierarchy and to ensure that everyone knows their seniority and therefore accords them the appropriate respect. Remember in Chapter 3 the importance of having your title on your business card was discussed? Your seniority is also reflected in the size and location of your office and whether you have a view or not; as Max found in Portugal too. Being related to someone important, or being a part of their inner circle, always affords advantages and respect. The offspring of well-connected communist party founders, who today hold so many positions of power and wealth, are often referred to as the 'Princelings of China' and these relationships are a key element of *guanxi*, as discussed in both Chapters 5 and 10.

> In Achievement oriented cultures, respect is not automatic but has to be earnt.

In Achievement oriented cultures, respect is not automatic but has to be earnt. Each individual must show by their proficiency and skill that they are deserving of both their position and the respect of others. Ascription can be a very difficult concept to deal with when working across cultures, as it appears to give an unfair advantage to someone who has not really done anything to deserve it. Achievement-oriented managers can feel very compromised by the acceptance, within an ascription culture, that senior managers sometimes have their positions due to their connections, rather than to their hard work and knowledge.

Michael, for example, was an Australian HR Manager who worked for a large construction company and came up against this issue.

His firm had recently set up an office in Bangkok and I was asked to provide some advice on integrating the two workforces. When we met, Michael had just heard that the Thai general manager, Sunan, had hired his brother-in-law to be the local HR manager and Michael was furious.

> *'He's not qualified for that role,' he fumed. 'I'm going to insist that he is sacked and I will oversee the new appointment instead.' Michael had a lot to learn not just about Ascription cultures, but also about the importance of 'face'. Sunan's brother-in-law had automatic status because of their relationship and if Michael had weighed in as he intended, it would have been disastrous. Sunan would have lost considerable face and would probably have made Michael's life very difficult afterwards. Michael would also have lost face in front of the other employees for having 'insulted' Sunan.*

A Western response was not going to work here, so the solution we opted for was to send Michael's assistant to Bangkok for a few weeks, to work alongside the new HR Manager and bring him up to speed. The cost of this was negligible in terms of the overall costs and the compromise afforded both Michael and Sunan an outcome they were happy with.

As with many of the cultural issues discussed so far and particularly the cultural dimensions, people are rarely all one way or the other. The USA, for example, is very much an Achievement culture, but it also considers titles to be very important, as anyone who has worked for an American firm with its preponderance of Vice Presidents would know. It is also common in America to bask in the reflected glory of a predecessor who has performed well, hence the popularity of names such as 'Mark Jackson the Third' or 'Mark Jackson Junior'. I have even seen someone on LinkedIn who describes herself as the great-granddaughter of a former American President.

Applying the Four R's

In this chapter we have considered the message that you are conveying via your clothes and your general appearance, even before you open your mouth to speak. Of course, this is true in your own culture to some extent too, but in your culture you know the 'rules' and are unlikely to turn up to the office in completely the wrong thing. Those jersey wrap-around dresses you love might not go down so well in a culture where, as a woman, you will struggle anyway to be taken seriously. As we saw in Chapter 4 too, when discussing verbal communication styles, the level of formality used in addressing colleagues varies hugely and we have to always be mindful of demonstrating the level of respect which is appropriate locally, given that person's place in the hierarchy. Finally, for all that we may feel that our client is just not up to the job, if he or she is related to the CEO we must just simply accept this inequity and get on with the job in hand. As an outsider, we must keep our judgements to ourselves.

How would you apply the **Four R's** to these issues?

Rewards

Questions:	There are many rewards inherent in making efforts in this area. What would some of them be for you?
Considerations:	Whatever position you hold, having comfortable relations with the people you work with will make you feel more relaxed. These relations may not be as friendly as you would like – remember Jack in Chapter 6, who got into trouble for sharing his break with the factory workers? – but it is more important

that they are culturally appropriate. Acting appropriately will make others feel more comfortable around you too, which inevitably will help in securing their support in achieving your outcomes.

Research

Questions:

How does the Achievemen vs Ascription dimension impact on some of the other anecdotes in this chapter? How would doing further reading about this help you to improve your relationships with some of the people you work with?

Considerations:

Once you understand how much this dimension can affect the outcome of your sales pitch or your efforts to build a relationship, then wear your best suit, use your Mont Blanc pen, admire his or her Louis Vuitton briefcase – and bond over the labels. It may sound very simplistic, but really, we all warm to people who share our values and this is just a very easy way to build a connection with someone. Remember too, the importance of titles and of people being seen to be respected in front of *their* colleagues or subordinates, at least until you have enjoyed a much longer relationship. Even then, your familiarity is not guaranteed to be welcome.

Reflect

Questions: Are you feeling a bit frustrated by what may seem like an imposition on your personal style? Not able to wear the clothes you prefer or to have the easy going relationship with your colleagues that you had before? Is this resentment showing at all and are you perhaps making arrows for your enemies to fire at you? There are always solutions, but they may not be immediately obvious; think about how Michael ended up resolving his issue in Thailand – how would you have dealt with that situation before reading this book? How would deal with it now?

Considerations: Make sure you don't leap too quickly to judge other people by your standards; what you might call obsequious (or a less polite phrase) may actually be perfectly acceptable behaviour in their culture. It's often not until we go somewhere new, that we really notice what we did at home and realise that our normal is not everybody else's. How does the etiquette in your overseas office differ from that at home and how comfortable are you with the differences? If something like having to modify your dress is annoying you, try to focus on the rewards you will get for fitting in. There are costs associated with any change and only you can decide if the costs outweigh the benefit.

Reach Out

Questions: This chapter is all about fitting in and getting on with people – how will you do it?

Considerations: Remember how quickly people will assess you; if you don't even *look* like you could fit in, how will you become accepted as one of the group? These first few weeks of your assignment or relationship are critical for you, so pay a lot of attention to rapport, as it incorporates many of the elements that this book has covered. Remember that rapport is about creating similarity and if you focus on this, both with regard to your appearance and the way that you interact with people, you will find that the rewards will soon follow.

Are there any other things to consider in light of what you've learnt from this chapter?

_____

_____

_____

_____

_____

References

- Narelle Hooper; http://www.afr.com/news/policy/industrial-relations/three-key-levers-for-business-success-20140905-jeqzu

- More about Charles Hampden-Turner and Fons Trompenaars' work can be seen at http://www.provenmodels.com/580/seven-dimensions-of-culture/charles-hampden-turner--fons-trompenaars

- http://www.forbes.com/sites/carolkinseygoman/2011/02/13/seven-seconds-to-make-a-first-impression/#2dc5cc70645a

10

Etiquette Matters
Wining, Dining &
Relationships

More often than not, our best relationships develop over a meal and with a glass of something in hand ...On your home turf and with clients from your own culture, these can be quite relaxing and enjoyable affairs. You both know what's expected, you're both familiar with the food and the format, you have plenty of topics to talk about – from sport to current affairs – and of course, you both know when is the 'right' time to steer the conversation round to business.

It's much the same with our work colleagues. 'At home' we know what's expected of us in terms of how much we socialise with our workmates, whether anyone will mind if we don't join them for lunch or how to behave if the boss joins us at the bar on Friday night after work.

All of these things and more are up for discussion when we start working across cultures. How important is it to join your Japanese client for karaoke? Do you really have to invite your Indian boss to your wedding? What on earth *is* footy tipping and why does it matter so much which team you support?

These all come down to two key issues; how do you make your client happy and how do you create a rewarding relationship with your new colleagues?

Connecting with Your Colleagues

To what extent can you expect your colleagues to become your friends? Obviously life is much more pleasant if people actually like each other, but there are also differences in cultural expectations around how much time colleagues are expected to spend together when outside of the office.

In Chapter 6 we discussed the concept of Work-Life Balance and the Western view that these two areas of people's lives should generally be kept quite separate. Of course, many people will become great friends with some of their colleagues – many people, like me, even *marry* their colleagues! – but generally office friendships in Western cultures are not deep and meaningful ones. For example, it is common for people to eat a sandwich at their desk and keep going with their work. This allows people to leave work earlier, but is viewed by people from other cultures as not only bad for the digestion, but not conducive to happy working relationships with your colleagues. In more group-orientated societies such as most of the Asian countries, colleagues will go out for lunch – often in quite large groups – and in the evenings may also have dinner together, to avoid the worst of the traffic before heading home. This provides not just a chance to have a break from work, but to spend time really getting to know the people they work with, so that they can be a real friend to them.

An Australian colleague who moved to China and thought he would continue to take lunch at his desk was soon 'corrected', as his wife Peta told me;

> My husband was told gently, but firmly, very early on by his wonderful Chinese assistant (I think possibly on his first day) that both bringing leftovers for lunch and eating at his desk was not appropriate for a manager at his level. From then on, he had to be seen to be taking his lunch break in the cafeteria, not warming up his leftovers in the work kitchenette – something his assistant told him managers did NOT do in China.

Unfortunately for all the millions of young Asians going to work in Anglo cultures, however, most people *don't* stop for lunch. Although several times a day, people will spend a few minutes chatting with colleagues while making themselves a coffee and so on, this is often not really long enough to have a meaningful conversation unless you already know the person or have things in common to start with. Without these opportunities, it can be very hard for newcomers from other cultures to feel like they are making any real kind of connection, so they often just end up befriending each other – and then being accused of being cliquey. But if everyone is talking about the football or the rugby and you don't know anything about this, why would you hang around? The pre-meeting small talk can be equally difficult to feel part of and one young Chinese woman confessed to me that the men talking sport made her feel "like a silly little girl, listening to

Unfortunately for all the millions of young Asians going to work in Anglo cultures, however, most people *don't* stop for lunch.

the grown-ups talking". In Australia, I always advise newcomers to pick a local sports team to follow, visit the website to learn the rules and always have a couple of highlights to contribute to a conversation. Even if you don't know much, your efforts will be appreciated.

In European cultures too, it is important not just to stop and spend time talking with your colleagues, but to take a moment to enjoy what is good in life – delicious food, fragrant coffee, a pleasant restaurant. Going out for lunch and for coffee with work colleagues is also an important stress-reliever in a hectic lifestyle, as Geert Hofstede observes;

In Italy the combination of high Masculinity and high Uncertainty Avoidance makes life very difficult and stressful. To release some of the tension that is built up during the day Italians need to have good and relaxing moments in their everyday life, enjoying a long meal or frequent coffee breaks.

As an aside, it's interesting to note that many European cars don't have cup holders, because driving to work while drinking your coffee would just add to your stress. Far better to enjoy some enjoyable 'conversazione' while drinking your cappuccino and start the day ten minutes later.

Marie, a French intern working in Sydney, was very put out by the lack of socialising in her office at lunchtime, as she wrote to her colleagues;

'For lunch, in France we are used to wait for each other and eat together. Here it's completely different. There is no canteen and most of the time you bring your own food from home. Many people eat in front of their computer! There is a kitchen where there is a microwave and a sandwich toaster to heat up your food, there are plates, glasses, cutlery and everything you may need. There is free coffee and biscuits and you can help yourself!! This is very unusual, and as a French person you feel very bad when you're eating alone in the kitchen!! Furthermore, for lunch Australians don't eat a lot, they will have a sandwich, or a soup but nothing very nourishing and when they see what you're having for lunch they are very surprised and always ask how such small person can eat so much.'

She also didn't like the alternative social of 'Friday Night Drinks', which is a popular time for colleagues to get together in Australia. The only female on the team, she personally found that many people drank too much, told her quite personal information which she was not comfortable hearing and yet expected a seamless return to 'business as usual' on Monday morning.

Even if going out to lunch or drinks after work is not your usual habit, it is wise to accept the local customs in matters like this, as it would be seen as very churlish to refuse an invitation. Note that if people of differing ranks do eat together (which in more hierarchical cultures is not the norm, but may happen occasionally) there is no expectation that the more senior person will pay. However, on holiday occasions such as Easter, Chinese New Year and Deepavali, it is much appreciated if a senior manager takes in a box of seasonal cakes or sweets for everyone to enjoy.

> In Australia, South Africans and Afrikaners have a reputation for being hard working and loyal, but also overly assertive and a bit serious.

In Australia or Britain, a senior manager joining younger staff for drinks after work may buy one round, but is likewise not expected to pay for everyone and it is also uncommon for them to stay for the whole evening. In France, younger staff like Marie would find it incredibly awkward if their boss joined them for drinks, but in many South American cultures this is not uncommon at all. In cultures where alcohol plays a big part in the relaxation process, it can also be challenging for people who don't drink to fit in. Of course they can join in for a few soft drinks, but many expatriates to Australia have commented to me that if they don't have a 'real' drink and don't loosen up in the same way as the others, not only do they feel a bit excluded from the social side but they also feel that their professional relationships suffer.

In Australia, South Africans and Afrikaners have a reputation for being hard working and loyal, but also overly assertive and a bit serious. A young Afrikans woman I know, 'Sonia', matched this stereotype perfectly and relocating was a very lonely time for her;

> Sonia had transferred with her company from Johannesburg to Melbourne. Her impression was that compared to South Africa, Australians were a bit too relaxed at work and spent too much time chatting to each other, instead of getting on with their work. Her habit in Johannesburg was to go straight to her desk and start working, so she continued to do this, even though she noticed that her colleagues usually chatted round the coffee machine for a while, a few times a

day. She quickly came to be seen as stand-offish by her colleagues, who now tended to ignore her, leaving her quite isolated.

Sonia was actually a lovely, warm young woman, but like many expatriates she came unstuck because she hadn't anticipated that in a different country, things would work differently. She probably wasn't helped by the reputation that South Africans have in Australia for being hard-working, but somewhat pushy and opinionated. Had she known of this view, she could have made extra effort to show that she wasn't like that.

Wining & Dining Dilemmas

Having got through a sometimes long and trying meeting with overseas clients, many Westerners at this point would happily go home if they could, or at least return to their hotel for room service. In Brazil, India, China, Russia and Malaysia, however – to name but a few predominately non-Western cultures – over the dinner table is where the relationship really starts getting some serious traction. Being invited to a meeting is merely an invitation to the *possibility* of a business discussion; business will not take place until both you and your company have proved themselves to be trustworthy, likeable and of suitable partnership material.

In any cultures like these, it's important to show that you are willing to enjoy good conversation and hospitality and even drinking games and karaoke on occasion. Making small but thoughtful gestures such as sending a gift for your clients' new baby, or a Chinese New Year card – even though you don't celebrate it – are all indicators that the friendship is valued, and only then might business follow. In new business meetings, a common mistake amongst more short-term-thinking Westerners is that they partake in a few minutes of small talk only and then try to get down to business. Given that in the early days the focus is on relationship building, in many countries business is barely discussed at all and it is easy to insult your host by starting to talk about the deal too soon. Meetings are where things go through the motions, between toasts and elaborate dishes is where business *friendships* are forged.

Rome wasn't built in a day and strong relationships will not be built at one meal either. Most Asians, Arabs and South Americans work on the basis of 'friendship first, business second' and the 'courtship' may take up to 12 or 18 months. There is an expectation that any hospitality provided will be reciprocated at another time and this is another occasion on which to remember the importance of face. The party who hosts the first dinner implies by their choice of venue how valuable the relationship is and the recipient should respond in kind, being careful not make the other party look cheap or feel slighted.

> As with the exchanging of gifts, being prepared to be generous with your *time* is an indication that the relationship is of value to you; people expecting to see quick results will be disappointed.

As with the exchanging of gifts, being prepared to be generous with your *time* is an indication that the relationship is of value to you; people expecting to see quick results will be disappointed. In most Western cultures, the focus is on getting the deal right and if a good relationship ensues, that's a bonus, but in other countries – including France, China, India, Chile and Nigeria – there should be no 'serious talk' until late in the meal – if at all. The thinking is that if a good *personal* relationship is established, then all parties will want what is most beneficial to that relationship and will therefore be less likely to do the wrong thing.

While of course, everyone would prefer to do business with people whose company they actively enjoy, in many South American cultures, people literally do business with people *first*. A buyer from a cosmetics company in California may have a great relationship with the company he buys his aloe vera from in Brazil, but if he leaves that company, his successor will literally have to start building a relationship from scratch. There will be goodwill, but nothing will be guaranteed until the new buyer has invested time building a new relationship.

Slurping & Burping

At lunches and dinners in all cultures there is a local protocol or accepted etiquette which it always pays to be aware of – not just so you don't embarrass yourself, but also so you don't make judgements too hastily about other people. A friend who does a lot of business in rural China recounted to me his horror at the "disgusting local table manners" of the people he dealt with – people belching, farting, talking with their mouths full and so on – but he had no concept whatsoever of judging their behaviour by *his* cultural standards. In China, Thailand, India and Turkey, burping after a meal shows both appreciation and satisfaction, and in Inuit communities, farting sends the same message. In Japan and Hong Kong, noisily slurping your noodles conveys not only how much you are enjoying them, but tells others how good they are too!

As Westerners, we are typically brought up to finish all the food on

> As Westerners, we are typically brought up to finish all the food on our plate, but in the Philippines, Thailand and Egypt, as well as many Asian cultures (*except* Japan), this suggests that the host has not provided enough food for you...

our plate, but in the Philippines, Thailand and Egypt, as well as many Asian cultures (*except* Japan), this suggests that the host has not provided enough food for you and you will soon find another helping in front of you. Likewise, the Western way of eating Chinese food is to accompany it with rice, but traditionally rice was used to bulk up the more expensive ingredients. At special occasions in China, therefore, asking your host for rice would be to imply that you are still hungry because he could not afford to provide enough quality food to fill you up with.

> **At most 'special occasion' meals, a range of delicacies will be offered to the guest of honour and they are not always to his or her taste …**

At most 'special occasion' meals, a range of delicacies will be offered to the guest of honour and they are not always to his or her taste … So how important is it to sample the sheep's eyeballs in Saudi Arabia or the duck's feet wrapped in chicken's intestines in Malaysia? The fermented mares milk in Mongolia or the eye-watering kimchi in Korea? The fried grasshoppers in Mexico, the horsemeat sashimi, the whale bacon in Japan or even the deep-fried tarantulas in Cambodia? The bad news is that it is usually considered insulting if you don't at least try it, but the good news is that you don't have to eat it all.

If you have dietary restrictions of some kind, or are vegetarian, be sure to advise your host beforehand. At special banquets and so on where a particular dish may be prepared for you in your capacity as honoured guest, it would cause your host great loss of face if you were not to eat it. A friend of mine who is a vegetarian and lives in Mongolia says that most of the time she is fine, but occasionally there is no avoiding the special dish. On one such occasion, she had been up in the country inspecting small-holdings; it was about minus 20 degrees outside and when she came in, she was presented with what was literally a bowl of liquid animal fat. She was however so *unbelievably cold,* that she not only devoured it but found it quite delicious!

Eating and drinking from the same plate or cup is not very likely to be something a business traveler will experience, but it can still happen. In Fiji, for example, a common welcome ceremony is for the island chief to welcome visitors with a bowl of *kava,* an alcoholic drink made from powdered plant roots. Not only can the thick brown liquid look and taste somewhat unappealing, it is traditionally served in a large bowl with a communal cup, which is passed around the group. It is always amusing to see a bunch of tourists wrestling with their consciences about how to avoid giving offence to the chief, yet also somehow avoid drinking the stuff and sharing a cup with 20 complete strangers!

While hiking in rural China, my husband and I stayed at a number of host farms and at mealtimes we always ate off a communal plate, which we shared with our male host and our guide. This involved leaning towards the plate and slurping, to try and avoid dropping food all over the table. From time to time our host would offer us special morsels off the end of his own chopsticks, directly into our mouths. The little bowls placed in front of us were strictly reserved for beer and luckily our inhibitions were relaxed by frequent topping up of the bowls and many cheery shouts of 'Gahn bay!' (Bottoms Up!) throughout the evening.

Westerners should always use chopsticks in Asia if they possibly can. Remember, however, that double-dipping with your chopsticks is considered extremely rude among more educated Chinese people and it

> ## Westerners should always use chopsticks in Asia if they possibly can.

is equally taboo to feed another person from your chopsticks or to leave your chopsticks sticking up in your rice bowl – the latter is done only at funerals.

Fingers & Forks

Don't be fooled into thinking that American and European cultures don't also have their foibles, which can trip people up just as easily. In Germany, it is insulting to the cook to suggest his or her potatoes are not soft enough to be cut with a fork, and in many areas of France, lettuce must never be cut with a knife and fork but instead, folded onto your fork. Many Americans will cut up all the food on their plate with a knife and fork, then proceed to eat it with the fork only, held in the right hand. People from some other cultures, however, regard this as somewhat childish behaviour. An American travel blog I found reminds travellers of the need for appropriate table manners while eating in Europe, including:

> *'Eating Continental style': In Europe, Continental style calls for handling your fork with your left hand (with the tines facing down!) and your knife in your right. Don't rest your elbows on the table, but don't allow your hands to rest under the table, out of sight.*

In India and neighbouring countries and throughout the Middle East, cutlery is often not used at all. Food feeds the soul as well as the body and a thorough enjoyment of the food includes enjoying the texture of it in your hand. Only the right hand is used to eat with, the left hand is for cleaning yourself with after visiting the toilet; it may be helpful to physically sit on your left hand to avoid inadvertently using it and of course giving great offence. This is one of those skills that looks so easy, but invariably leads to sauce on your tie or rice stuck to your arm, so it would be wise to practice before you go. When eating with your hands, it is of course essential that they be clean; a dish of water will often be brought to the table so that everyone can effectively demonstrate that their hands *are* clean.

As David Livermore points out in his book *Expand Your Borders,* one of the other reasons cutlery is not used in some cultures is that in the past, knives and forks had the potential to double as weapons. Chopsticks originated in Confucius' time, as he felt that having knives at the table was not conducive to a harmonious atmosphere (importance of harmony *again)* and that 'violent' acts such as butchering meat should be done out of sight. Knives are still rarely seen on tables in Asian countries as they continue to be associated with violence. In Thailand, a fork is never used to put food into your mouth, but only to push food on to your spoon.

What Time is Dinner?

Both the time you go to dinner and the time you spend eating dinner can vary enormously. In North America, dinner time typically starts between 6 and 8 pm. and an average business dinner might last a couple of hours. But in South America, many restaurants do not even open until 8 p.m. and it is not uncommon to eat at 10 or 11 p.m. In India too, dining is usually 8 o'clock at the earliest and may be as late as 10.30 p.m. while in Saudi Arabia, formal dinners can start at 11 p.m. or even midnight. These meals often consist of many courses, served over a long period of time.

These late dinners can be very challenging for business travelers trying to contend with long hours and jet-lag, as Susie recalls from an evening in Dubai:

'My client told me he wanted to show me what Dubai used to be like,' she told me, *'so we went out into the desert to this recreated "camp",* where there were camel rides, belly dancing and traditional foods

served. It was beautiful, but it was incredibly hot and we sat about on wool carpets while an endless supply of dishes kept appearing. I really thought I was going to pass out! All I wanted was just to lie down for five minutes, but of course that was impossible …'

In Vino Veritas

> In countries which rely heavily both on their networks and on the value of face, your own reputation can be seriously compromised by doing business with the wrong person.

The purpose of spending time together on the golf course or at the dinner table is not just to be 'social'. In countries which rely heavily both on their networks and on the value of face, your own reputation can be seriously compromised by doing business with the wrong person. There is a not unreasonable belief, firmly bedded in the *In Vino Veritas* ('in wine, truth') school of thought, that how you behave after a few glasses of wine is a much more reliable indicator of your real self than your business persona is. If you are indiscreet, or say something derogatory about your colleagues or the company you work for, you may be sure there will be a black mark against your name. It is common amongst the Chinese to have numerous toasts raised and to essentially play drinking games and see if someone can be tricked into either saying the wrong thing or letting something slip. It is considered rude to avoid these endless toasts, so many Westerners will excuse themselves due to 'allergies' or 'ill health' – the Chinese must find Westerners to be a very unhealthy lot. Some senior Chinese businessmen will even occasionally have people who drink *for them*.

A number of toasts will almost certainly be raised at these special dinners and it is a good idea to come prepared to respond. Even a few words of the local language goes a long way, as does of course being gracious, modest and giving your host face.

In Muslim cultures, of course, alcohol is less common. Alcohol is deemed forbidden by the Qur'an, so in theory no alcohol will be consumed at all during business dinners and lunches, but as in all things there are exceptions. In Oman for example, a man is allowed to consume alcohol in a public place, so long as his head is covered by either a *kuma* (cap) or *massar* (turban). It is certainly best practice to assume that alcohol will *not* be allowed, as it is always far better to play it safe, but I have heard many examples of alcohol being consumed at private dinners and in fact experienced this myself;

> *Many years ago I had reason to entertain a Pakistani vice-consul and his wife at our home in London. An aide had asked me (instructed, actually) to buy whisky for the vice-consul to drink, but when they arrived he told me his wife did not consume alcohol. This was long before I had even thought about cultural differences and I had created a lavish three-course meal for them, with every dish soaked in alcohol as was the vogue in the 1980s. Thinking of my menu, I quickly made an executive decision not to say anything about it. His wife was certainly very relaxed that night…*

In January 2016, a delegation of Iranian ministers visited both Italy and France. In Italy, many of the nude statues around the hall were given drapes of one sort or another, to preserve their modesty. On arriving in France, it was requested of President François Hollande that he refrain from serving alcohol at the planned lunch, not just to the Iranian guests but to everyone present. President Rouhani also requested that all the meat be *halal*. Hollande happily complied with the latter, but he refused not to serve wine on the basis that wine was far more than just alcohol to the French and was indeed one of their great cultural traditions. He offered to host a 'high tea' as an alternative and it remains to be seen whether his actions will adversely affect the French-Iranian relationship, but it prompted much discussion about whose responsibility it was to accommodate the other.

Adam Gopnik wrote very persuasively in *The New Yorker* about this incident:

> *Trivial as it might seem, the dispute touches on a real issue, worth pursuing: what is owed to guests who see the world differently? How extensive are the duties of hospitality, which incline us to think that we should do all in our power to make our guests feel comfortable and at home, providing them minimal embarrassment or awkwardness? And, against that, what is owed according to the duties of integrity— not pretending to our guests that we are in any way ashamed or unwilling to stand up for our own values, even while respecting theirs?*

Gopnik goes on to make a great case for both parties having legitimate points of view but that, in the end, finding a way to compromise is always going to be the best outcome. In summary, he writes;

> *We always reach out to strangers across a table of misunderstanding. Moral clarity is good; but muddled concord is usually better. The best thing to do, as the diplomats say, is to find a formula. "Pass the wine," one President could have said, and "I'll pass on the wine," the other could have replied—and the tiny difference, barely registered, might*

have made all the difference. It is of such small harmonies that lasting peace is made.

Taboo Topics

So, you're all gathered round the Korean Barbeque or the restaurant table and you don't want to talk about business (yet, or at all on this occasion), so what do you talk about? I mentioned in an earlier chapter that doing some research into things that were of interest to locals or a source of pride to them, would always be appreciated, but there are also some topics to avoid. These vary from country to country, so you really have to do your local research, but it is usually a safe bet to avoid anything too contentious or anything that sounds remotely like a criticism of your host or your guest's country. It's hard, however, to generalise and say 'no politics' or 'no religion', as in some cultures your dining partners will welcome a well thought out argument, even if they don't agree with you. In France, for example, people will freely discuss their politics and even who they are voting for, whereas this is very uncommon in the Anglo cultures.

In Western cultures, it is generally still perceived as a bit inappropriate to talk about money too soon, and certainly salaries are never, ever discussed, even among friends. However, it is not uncommon in dealings with potential Asian clients to talk about money very early in the conversation, rather than first discussing in more detail what services can be offered. A Chinese woman whom I met with recently, to discuss a possible partnership, told me within ten minutes of meeting how much she

> In Western cultures, it is generally still perceived as a bit inappropriate to talk about money too soon, and certainly salaries are never, ever discussed, even among friends.

earned for her workshops and therefore how much she thought we could charge. As an Airbnb host, I find that Chinese guests will often ask the cost of the house, the car, the school fees and even the dogs. While living in Singapore, I was often astounded by the enquiries of retail assistants; when trying on clothes or shoes, for example, they would often ask questions about how where I lived, how much rent I paid, how much my husband earned and so on.

Maggie, who lived in China for ten years, had many similar experiences and confided to me that;

> *In my 10 years in Asia I never got used to this. I just couldn't feel comfortable discussing personal monetary matters like rent costs or the cost of my clothes with anyone who asked (and everyone did!). It always made me wince internally. What I did do, though, was develop ways of dealing with the questions. In the end, I could see the money question coming from a mile off! My response ranged from ignoring the question altogether, feigning misunderstanding and vaguely rabbiting on about something else, or just politely laughing and explaining that in my culture we didn't discuss money questions like that. In this regard, I couldn't change them, they couldn't change me, so I developed my own strategies to get me through.*

Many cultures can also be shockingly racist and sexist and as a visitor, it is usually most diplomatic to just let these comments pass. A 2016 TV advertisement in China, for example, showed a young black man being put into a washing machine and reappearing as a 'clean' young Asian man. The ad received widespread global condemnation and has now been removed, but initially the Chinese felt the Western media was being 'over sensitive'. How would you respond if your Chinese client showed you the ad of his phone over dinner, while laughing uproariously?

Finally, although it does seem like a stereotype, many French men do regard complimenting a woman on her hair and clothing as an obligatory expression of 'la courteoisie', an inconsequential combination of chivalry and courtesy. Many women will quite enjoy this flattery as, in my experience, most French men can pull this off without being sleazy. In the rather litigious USA, however, this type of flirtatious banter can attract a sexual harassment charge.

Building Lasting Relationships

Hug or Handshake?

As your relationship progresses, the 'body language' between you and your client may change and become warmer. In most countries, kissing and hugging can be a bit of a minefield and is hugely dependent on the strength of the relationship, the sex of the kissers and even the geographical location. The issue is not only whether to kiss or not, but how and how many times? Even in a professional setting, kisses can include lips to cheek, cheek to cheek and even lips to lips if people are well known to each other.

> As your relationship progresses, the 'body language' between you and your client may change and become warmer.

Australians are regarded by others as quite big on hugs, but not everyone shares their enthusiasm for them. I know of several Muslim women there who have spoken of their need to develop a 'straight-armed hug' which allows them to both honour their religious customs, but also to engage in the spirit of the occasion.

A few years ago I met a young Indian-Australian man who had recently returned to Australia;

When Dilip returned to Melbourne after working in Chile for several years, Australian men seemed very 'blokey'. His Chilean boss would greet him with a hug every morning at work, so when Dilip's colleague in Australia announced that his wife was expecting twins, he went over and gave him a hug – clearly much to the surprise of his other workmates, who only offered hearty handshakes.

In France and Belgium, two kisses is de rigueur, but in the Netherlands it is always three, and in some cultures it is even four – and it can depend if you are in the north or the south of that country. In France, male work colleagues will shake hands with everyone in their department every morning and will often exchange kisses with female colleagues, but *never* hugs. In Portugal, men will generally only kiss someone of the opposite sex – unless it's a family member – but in neighbouring Spain and in a number of South American countries, it is not uncommon for men to kiss each other.

Rebecca went to work in Brussels and was taken by surprise when other expats adopted the local manners. 'I expected the Belgians to kiss me on the cheek,' she said, 'but I was once so surprised by an English man in Brussels who went for the '2 kiss on the cheeks' farewell that I ended up kissing his glasses ... He was a client, so it was particularly awkward!'

In some South American cultures, people offer a hug or a clasp but only an 'air kiss'. In Brazil it is common for two women, or a man and a woman, to kiss each other upon being introduced, but in Germany kisses are reserved for very close colleagues. In China and India, kisses are definitely for the bedroom only and kisses on the lips are not allowed at all in Bollywood films. In the Philippines, cheek-to-cheek kissing is the way to go, but it is seen as something only members of the upper class do; most Filipinos would only kiss family members. In the UK, a double kiss on the cheeks amongst colleagues, clients and friends is now fairly common amongst professional people, but is by no means universal there and is seen by some as merely imitating the French habit and therefore being a bit of an affectation.

Guanxi

Anyone who has tried to do business in China will be familiar with the concept of *guanxi*; the topic was introduced in Chapter 5 as part of the discussion about maintaining harmony. *Guanxi* describes what we would refer to in Western cultures as our 'network' or 'relationships' but in China it signifies much more than this. In addition to the qualities that are required of any trading partner – being able to deliver a good quality product, to an agreed price, by an agreed time – having the right connections is critical to success. The concept of *guanxi* is largely about having a group of *trusted* people who can be wholly relied upon not only to support each other, but also to protect the integrity of the group as a whole and to maintain the harmony. It is in many ways a risk-mitigation strategy; there is a sense of mutual obligation within the group, but also one of assured loyalty. It takes a long time to establish your *guanxi* and not surprisingly, it is especially difficult for non-Chinese to gain access to these

> It takes a long time to establish your *guanxi* and, not surprisingly, it is especially difficult for non-Chinese to gain access to these groups...

groups, as they have no shared history and therefore have not built up a reputation for being trustworthy. Non-Chinese can only be part of this 'inner circle' by being introduced to the group by a current member and this will only happen when that person feels completely confident that the stranger will not cause damage to the group. That confidence is gained by spending a lot of time together, seeing how you behave and assessing whether you will be a harmonious addition to the group or a disruptive one.

Being part of the network assumes acceptance of the 'code of conduct' and a willingness to accept this mutual obligation. As David Livermore describes it in his book *Expand Your Borders*:

> *Guanxi is sometimes regarded by outsiders as Chinese xenophobia or cronyism, because it is built on the idea of giving preferential treatment to insiders. Although guanxi can be abused, it is, at heart, simply a mode of relationship ... Many Individualistic cultures thrive on talking about relationships that have no strings attached [but] from a Confucian perspective, a relationship without strings attached is not a relationship. Friendship and familial relationships are built upon commitment and the expectation that there will be reciprocal commitment.*

Although not to the same extent, these kind of relationships do of course exist everywhere, with nepotism being the ultimate example of supporting your network.

Client Service Expectations

As has been demonstrated though a number of different anecdotes, many non-Western clients have a very different expectation of client servicing. Relationships are established slowly and on the whole it is hoped that they will last a long time. For this to happen, people have to know each well, so need to work and socialize together. The first meeting for most people is like a first date in a possible romance; it sets the tone for the relationship. A firm of Canadian architects hoping to secure a project in India, for example, would be wasting their time if they only allowed for a presentation and a business meeting and then planned to fly home that night. An Australian firm who only provided coffee at a first meeting with a potential Taiwanese client would similarly be perceived as not really showing the appropriate level of interest. A German sales manager who didn't factor in both a late night dinner and probably a game of golf too while visiting his client in Brazil would very possibly go home empty-handed.

> The first meeting for most people is like a first date in a possible romance; it sets the tone for the relationship.

Libby was a buyer for a cosmetics company in Australia and confessed to me that she was finding one of her suppliers of cocoa butter in Venezuela very difficult to work with. In phone calls and emails, everything was promised, but delivery was another matter altogether and Libby was getting more and more frustrated. Her predecessor had set up the relationship and didn't seem to have had nearly so many setbacks, but he had actually visited Venezuela, something Libby didn't have a budget for until the following year.

My feeling was that her supplier did not really feel a personal connection to Libby so, knowing how important that was to many South Americans, we discussed how she could improve this. A week later she told me that they were now friends on Facebook and that she had also Skyped him from home one night, not just so that they could have an almost face-to-face, but also so that he could meet her little boys. They had both agreed that Skyping was much friendlier and had diarised another call, this time so that Libby could say a virtual 'hello' to his children too. Delivery improved significantly.

Your mother, in helping you to plan your love life, may have advised you to 'Treat 'em mean and keep 'em keen' but that approach wouldn't work in much of Asia or South America. Many Westerners, however, would much rather catch up over a quick coffee than a long lunch and would prefer to go to the gym at lunchtime or leave a bit earlier at the end of the day than spend time being wined and dined. This is *their* normal but that doesn't mean it is everyone else's too.

Matthew is a lawyer in Perth I know, whose company had recently started working with a Singaporean client. I happened to meet him at a networking function and he asked me if I could explain why after the first meeting, their client had written to say that 'despite the disappointing nature of our first meeting with you, we are prepared to commit to a one-month trial'. Matthew had no idea what difficulties his client was referring to, as from his point of view, the meeting had gone well – they had got the business hadn't they? We caught up a few days later and I went through all the likely culprits.

> *Had they exchanged gifts? Yes, but the Australians hadn't wrapped theirs. Were they familiar with the etiquette around the handling of business cards? No, they hadn't really looked at them. Had they observed appropriate hierarchy in terms of seating more senior people at the same end of the table, near to each other? They hadn't suggested that everyone be on first name terms, had they? Or addressed questions directly to the more junior managers, rather than letting the senior person delegate? But hopefully things went well over dinner? Ah, there had been no client dinner …*

As Matthew had failed in every one of these areas, it was remarkable that they got the business at all, but it can of course happen that way. Sometimes you have what they need and they will overlook your shortcomings, but it doesn't generally pave the way for a lasting relationship – how could it?

Lucy is Chinese and is the team leader at an investment bank in Melbourne. She had a number of high net-worth Chinese clients who were considering using her bank's services, largely thanks to the relationships she herself had established with them over many months. However, they now also wanted to meet her colleagues and this was creating an issue. On visits to Melbourne the clients' idea of customer service included being taken to the zoo on Sunday, or out for dinner on a Saturday night – in other words, socialising with the people they were trusting their money to – but as far as her Australian team was concerned, this was quite beyond their remit.

Author Richard D Lewis recounts a story in *Business Insider* magazine, of a top American insurance salesman named Simpson, who was sent on an expatriate assignment to Japan. It provides an extraordinary example of the level of client servicing that can be expected in a culture which views it as a privilege to be of service.

In the article, Lewis explains that after six weeks in Japan, Simpson had not managed to close a single sale – was he losing his touch or did he just need to find a different strategy to use? His American manager provided some cultural training for him by way of sending him out on some sales calls with the company's top Japanese salesman, Ichiro Harada, to see if Simpson noticed anything different about the way he worked. They visited a key client, Mr Watanabe and afterwards Simpson was full of questions;

Simpson's questions were both to the point: Why had Harada not even mentioned the account and why had Watanabe given him a set of keys?

> *Harada smiled indulgently as he explained, "There was no need to mention business, as the account remains secure, as long as I say nothing than [sic] displeases President Watanabe. As he likes baseball and is a keen golfer, these subjects, as well as some others, are safe ground for discussion. I support the same baseball team and my golf handicap is inferior to his. I never talk about anything that might be controversial. A half hour's chat like this one, once a month, gives him occasions [sic] for relaxation. Normally he has to work 10-12 hour days and he welcomes this type of break. He cannot be bothered by strangers coming into his office trying to sell him insurance".*

And the car keys? They were handed over so that Harada could take Mr Watanabe's wife to the shopping mall that afternoon. She didn't drive or use public transport, so relied on her husband to drive her. By taking her himself, Harada would allow his client to enjoy a quiet Sunday either at home or on the golf course.

Customer service indeed and worth remembering next time you are endeavouring to secure a new client in a culture not your own. Not that everyone would expect this level of customer service, but there are many degrees of it and if you can match your delivery to their expectations, your relationship should run much more smoothly.

Applying the Four R's

As with all of the topics discussed in this book, managing the differences becomes so much easier when you know what the differences are and you have thought about how to manage them. Realistically, few people will ever be able to perform to quite the same standard in someone else's culture as they do in their own, but it's always good to have something to strive for!

Hopefully by this stage of the book, you've recognised the value of preparation and research and you feel a lot more confident about your ability to build some great cross-cultural partnerships. However, confidence is a fickle friend. What do you do at those times when you just can't bear the thought of another Chinese banquet, when you're despairing of ever getting the contract signed and you're miserable and homesick? Because that's going to happen too, so below are just a few strategies to help deal with those days.

Rewards

Questions:
Rewards come in all shapes and sizes but sometimes we get so caught up in our problems that we forget to think about them at all. If this is where you are now, struggling to see the rewards, how can you make it easier for yourself?

Considerations:
Review the kind of rewards you are hoping for; maybe it is time to switch your focus. Have long and short-term goals so that you have some sense of achievement. Look outside of your work for ways to get rewarded through volunteering and so on. Help someone else. Think long-term, where might this one dinner or one day at the races take you? Use the event as a challenge for yourself; keep it interesting by seeing what you can learn.

Research

Questions: What's your biggest concern right now and what's the outcome you want? What do you need to know, in order to secure that outcome?

Considerations: Whatever your concern is, you won't be the first person to struggle with it, so there is an answer out there somewhere! Make a list of people who can help you; other expats? Colleagues? A professional expat coach or trainer? Feeling out of control is the single biggest factor in stress creation, so get specific, make a plan and get back in control.

Reflect

Questions: Are you feeling a bit like Lucy's Australian colleagues at the moment – a bit resentful? A bit fed up with having to accommodate these cultural differences all the time? Do you think the Iranians in the French wine issue should just put up and shut up? Are you just going to eat at your desk if you want to and not care what other people think?

Considerations: Actually, it's perfectly understandable to feel like that sometimes, so don't beat yourself up about it. In the same way that you can have a great game of golf one day and play poorly the next, working across cultures definitely has its high and low points and there is no point in pretending otherwise. If you are an expatriate, make sure you have regular time out when you don't have to think about all these things so you can recharge your batteries. Try to be more accepting of your situation; ask yourself if it's really going to matter in a year or even a month's time. Try hard to take the personal out of it and just accept it as a task that needs completing but will soon be over. Focus on your rewards.

Reach Out

Questions: You might be feeling so fed up that it doesn't seem like there is any point in even trying to connect with anyone else. But review the strategies listed in Chapter 2; have you really tried them all? What do others do that seems to work?

Considerations: How much more frustrated and miserable do you think you will feel if you don't talk to anyone about this issue? If you bottle it all up and don't resolve it? If you discover later that there was a solution, if only you'd asked someone else instead of assuming? If you'd been really honest with yourself and with others? If you'd been just a bit more flexible and not jumped to conclusions? You have a lot of the answers already, you just need to give yourself a bit of space and let 'la vie s'arrange' as the French would say. ('Life will take care of itself')

Are there any other things to consider in light of what you've learnt from this chapter?

References

- http://www.healthytravelblog.com/2012/08/10/travel-etiquette-part-3-eating-without-embarrassing-yourself/

- http://www.newyorker.com/news/daily-comment/france-iran-and-the-affair-of-the-lunch-wine

- Richard Lewis is quoted in Business Insider; http://www.businessinsider.com/salesmen-in-the-us-and-japan-2014-5?IR=T

- David Livermore, *Expand Your Borders,* Cultural Intelligence Centre LLC, Michigan 2013,pp57-62

- https://geert-hofstede.com/italy.html

- Chinese laundry ad https://www.youtube.com/watch?v=Xq-I0JRhvt4 (may no longer be available as company has tried to remove all links)

Summary

In his book *The Art of Travel*, author and philosopher Alain de Botton describes overhearing some people talking on a bus, complaining about not being understood and other people not being efficient. He writes how he then

> … *thought of the similarities of complaints – always selfishness, always blindness – and the old psychological truth that what we complain of in others, others will complain of in us.*

In other words, it's always the other person's fault and it is the other person's responsibility to change. Simply put, 'they' must become more like 'us'. As an English child growing up in Belgium and then America, I learnt another way, which was far less limiting than this attitude.

In Belgium, from the age of nine to fifteen, my three particular friends in the neighbourhood were Dutch, Italian and French – Liesel, Simonetta and Pascal. We all learnt to speak a little of each other's languages and in a completely unplanned way, we all learnt about each other's cultures; that Simonetta ate something called spaghetti on a regular basis, that Liesel got an 'extra Christmas' on Saint Nicholas' day and that Pascal had to go to the bakery at 5 p.m. every day, to buy a fresh baguette for the evening meal. He also got to drink wine, even though he was only nine! I'm sure they learnt about some English oddities from visiting my house too (like baked beans on toast and pink and yellow Battenberg cake), but none of it mattered in the slightest, so long as everyone could ride a bike, kick a ball or enjoyed going to the local funfair.

Without thinking about it, when we moved into the neighbourhood I had put the **Four R's** into practice, (undoubtedly with some input from my parents):

Firstly, I thought about my **Rewards**: What did I want? That was easy, friends in the neighbourhood to play with.

Next I did some **Research**: How would I meet them? Where to find them? I went out into the street and found both boys and girls of my age, who seemed friendly enough, but none of them spoke English and I didn't yet speak French.

I then **Reflected** on the problem: There weren't any other English kids in my street, so I would have to be flexible and try something different. These kids were already friends too, which meant I needed them more than they needed me. So, the effort would mostly have to be on my part.

How then could I **Reach Out**? I'm sure it wasn't really strategic on my part, but I learnt that there were things I could do which helped. I found that bearing gifts – particularly chocolate and biscuits – was a great door opener. I showed a willingness to put myself last: I let other kids ride my bike or I'd go in goal when nobody else wanted to. I asked them to teach me their language(s) and I helped them with their English homework. We found that we had something to offer each other and friendships ensued.

It may sound simplistic, but this was my 'normal' from quite an early age; people did things differently to me, but so what? That didn't mean we couldn't be friends. If I had let it, the language barrier in particular could have prevented me from ever being part of the gang in Avenue Cinq Bonniers, but I chose not to let it.

Although only young, I had learnt that differences only really matter if we let them. If, when meeting people from other cultures we focus on what we could share in the future and on what we have in common already, we will find the cultural gaps are not impossible to bridge after all. And that if we reach our hand out, there will almost always be someone willing to take it.

Alain de Botton, *The Art of Travel,* 2002, Penguin Books, p. 252

Join the Conversation!

If you have a favourite cultural moment to share, or a story in this book jogs a memory, please share it! Perhaps you would like to post a photo of yourself, reading this book in some exotic location?

You can join in the conversation on Facebook at https://www.facebook.com/CulturalChemistrytheBook/

Additional Resources

In addition to being the name of the book, **Cultural Chemistry** is also the name of the author's business. A range of expatriate coaching, cross-cultural training, seminars and public speaking services are offered, incorporating the **Four R's** approach. These can also be combined with the **CQ Assessment**, a tool developed by the Cultural Intelligence Centre (www.culturalQ.com) and suitable for use by both individuals and groups.

For further information, or to post your review or comments, please visit or contact me:

- By email: patti@culturalchemistry.com.au

- Via the website: www.culturalchemistry.com.au

- Or via the Facebook page:
  https://www.facebook.com/CulturalChemistrytheBook/

- Via LinkedIn: Patti McCarthy (Hewstone)

- Using the Twitter handle: @CultureChemist

Recommended Reading

Gurnek Bains, *Cultural DNA*, Wiley, New Jersey, 2015

Andy Molinsky, *Global Dexterity*, Harvard Business Review Press, Boston, 2013

David Livermore, *The Cultural Intelligence Difference*, American Mgt Assoc, New York, 2011

David Livermore, *Expand Your Borders,* Cultural Intelligence Centre LLC, Michigan 2013

Tom Verghese, *The Invisible Elephant*, Synergistic Press, 2006

Fons Trompenaars & Charles Hampden-Turner, *Riding the Waves of Culture,* Brealey, London 2011

Terri Morrison & Wayne A Conaway, *Kiss, Bow or Shake Hands*, Adams Media, Avon MA, 1995

Geert Hofstede, Gert Jan Hofstede & Michael Minkov, *Cultures and Organizations*, McGraw-Hill Books, USA, 2010

Geert Hofstede, *Culture's Consequences,* SAGE Publications, California,1984

Richard D Lewis, *When Cultures Collide,* Brealey, London, 1996 (Revised 2006)

Edward T Hall, *Beyond Culture*, Anchor Books, 1977

Barry Tomalin & Mike Nicks, *The World's Business Cultures and how to Unlock Them*, Thorogood, London, 2010

David C Thomas & Kerr Inkson, *Cultural Intelligence,* Berrett-Koehler, San Francisco, 2003

Michelle T. Johnson *The Diversity Code*, American Mgt Assoc, New York, 2011

Recommended Websites

Most of the above have websites also. The ones listed below are very useful for pre-trip research; many have free country guides, webinars and so on. These are just a start...

www.communicaid.com

www.kwintessential.co.uk

www.worldbusinessculture.com

www.dfat.gov.au/geo/pages/countries-and-regions.aspx

www.gov.uk/government/collections/exporting-country-guides

www.commisceo-global.com

www.aperianglobal.com

www.justlanded.com

Ease of Doing Business Index: http://data.worldbank.org/indicator/IC.BUS.EASE.XQ

www.expatica.com

www.internations.org

The author is a regular media commentator and there are a number of interviews available to listen to at: www.culturalchemistry.com.au/MEDIA

Special thanks to Ian Scott of IS Design for the black and white illustrations. Ian can be contacted at
Design IS: ian@designis.com.au

To purchase further copies of this book please;

- Visit www.culturalchemistry.com.au and follow the link

- Phone 1300 862663 (within Australia)

- Ask for it at your local book shop

- Purchase it in hard copy or e-book format from a range of online booksellers including Amazon, Book Depository, Barnes & Noble, Kobo and Apple iTunes.